meals in any city await – so often overlooked. Why, in a city like Athens, with such rich culinary districts, are these areas and their bounty of good food so rarely explored and celebrated?

In response, we launched Culinary Backstreets™, devoted to collecting the best undiscovered local eateries you might not always find on your own. We're talking serious food for serious eaters, hold the frills.

Beyond souvlaki – and what you will find listed in most guidebooks – lies a wide range of unique Greek regional cuisines and restaurants with hints of Mediterranean, Turkish and Middle Eastern cooking.

With this booklet as your trusty introduction to the culinary backstreets of Athens, you will know what to eat and where to eat it.

Because prices tend to change, we have decided to generally not include them in our reviews. Most of the spots covered vary from very inexpensive to modest. More importantly, we consider all of our selections high in value. Alcohol is ordinarily among the offerings, unless otherwise indicated in the review. In general, we recommend making reservations for dinner.

Welcome to Athens's Culinary Backstreets,
Kali Orexi!

Ansel Mullins & Yigal Schleifer
Founders, Culinary Backstreets

CONTENTS

DOWNTOWN

AMA LACHI STIS NEFELIS

Άμα Λάχει - Στης Νεφέλης
Address: Kallidromiou 69, Exarchia
Telephone: +30 384 5978
Hours: Mon-Fri, 10am-11:30pm;
       Sat-Sun, 11am-11:30pm
       (lunch starts at 1pm)

School Lunch (and Dinner)

Set in a hidden oasis of fragrant lemon trees, geraniums, bougainvillea and jasmine, Ama Lachi Stis Nefelis (If by Chance at Nefeli's) holds the unusual distinction of being the former public primary school of Exarchia.

Children still sit at the tables at this modern *mezedopoleio,* but nowadays, they're joined by their families. The crowd is usually young here and includes intellectuals, university students, hipsters and couples, all enjoying the casual, vibrant atmosphere.

The kitchen really gets going at 1 p.m., turning out traditional Greek dishes with a modern slant, such as baked chickpeas with smoked pork and *horta* (wild greens) and pureed fava (yellow split peas) with fennel root and mixed nuts. We recommend the smoked eggplant with Cretan galotyri cheese and grilled pita bread, the *mizithropitakia* (Cretan-style mini pies with mizithra cheese, honey, mint and sesame seeds), the selection of traditional sausages from around Greece and the grilled talagani cheese served with tomato marmalade. We also love the fried meatballs with ouzo and fresh mint served with yogurt on the side and the delightfully crispy, hand-cut fried potatoes.

There's a great selection of house and bottled wine, tsipouro from Tyrnavos, tsikoudia from Crete, ouzo from Lesvos and beers from all over Greece to enjoy along with your meal. As far as desserts go, we've got two favorites: sour cherry semifreddo topped with a seasonal fruit salad and *mastiha* (mastic) syrup and then the *ekmek kataifi* with mastiha cream and whipped cream on top.

The tables in the enchanting stone-paved courtyard are first come, first served, but reservations can be made for the tables inside. Evenings are generally busy from 9 p.m. onwards, and Sundays during lunchtime are crowded too. Service is not the speediest, but there's no need to rush through the food and drink here – this is a classroom meant for lingering.

AVLI

Αυλή
Address: Agiou Dimitriou 12, Psyri
Telephone: +30 210 321 7642
Hours: Wed-Mon, 12:30pm-2am

Funky House of Meatballs

Avli is one of those places you have to be introduced to by someone who's already been there. Although a sign does exist above its narrow metal door, there's so much graffiti on either side of it, you could walk right by even if you had the address firmly in your hand or mind. Avli means "courtyard," but this one is narrow, much more like a back alley.

Funky is the word that comes to mind, an impression reinforced when you examine the faded clippings, drawings and magazine ads hanging on the walls and pasted on the shutters (all gifts from friends), the cracked marble flagstones, the small tables with their plastic "cloths" of different colors, stripes, checks or flowers, the somewhat bedraggled garland of garlic and chili peppers hanging from a drainpipe.

But the simple menu boasts some of Athens's best *keftedakia* (succulent meatballs, with a crisp crust and a moist, meltingly soft interior), an omelet studded with *pastourma* and

cheese, fry-ups of chicken, liver or pork with peppers, a *poikilia* (assortment) of mezedes, *spetzofai* (sausage, pepper and onion casserole), cabbage rolls with egg-lemon sauce, and very drinkable box wines.

It's amazing that so much good food comes out of such a small kitchen. We've seen bigger on modest yachts. And yet, Takis Stamatelopoulos, who started working here in the mid-1980s and now owns the place, says it's a fairly recent addition. "Before that, we even cooked in the courtyard." He shows us a photo.

Whatever his secret, he has the right recipe. Avli has a firm following of local and foreign customers. The food is authentic Greek home style, the prices very reasonable and the atmosphere casual and cozy. You would not come here for haute cuisine, candlelight and linen napkins, but if it's backstreet fare you're looking for, a peek into traditional Athens, you will be happy you stepped through that camouflaged door.

COOKOOMELA GRILL

Cookoomèla Grill
Address: 43 Themostokleous Street, Exarchia
Telephone: +30 21 1182 2343
Hours: Mon-Thurs, 1pm-11pm;
       Fri-Sat, 1pm-midnight

Souvlaki Iconoclasts

In the center of Exarchia, a hub of activism often referred to as the "anarchist" neighborhood of Athens, a small minimalist eatery with just a few tables outside opened in April 2018 – becoming an instant success by breaking all the rules. At first glance, it looks like a regular souvlaki shop, with sauces and condiments lined up at the front, pita breads being grilled and potatoes being fried. It even smells familiar. But if you look closely, you will notice that there is no meat in sight or, to be exact, no animal products. Welcome to Cookoomela Grill, Greece's first vegan souvlaki spot.

It takes a lot of courage to transform the most emblematic meat-based street food in Greece – one that Greeks adore – into a meat-free version. "We couldn't have opened anywhere else apart from Exarchia. It is a very open-minded, free neighborhood that welcomes and supports new ideas. In my opinion, it is the most vegan-friendly place in Greece," says owner Antonis Margaritis. But he admits that they did not expect such sudden fame, even in such an alternative neighborhood. Greeks are genuine meat lovers, so there is some stigma associated with refraining from eating meat, even though traditional Greek cuisine features countless vegan recipes.

"Cookoomela" is slang in Greece's Epirus and Thessaly regions for the morchella mushroom, a fitting name for a place that uses mushrooms as the main ingredient in their souvlaki. Grilled dark and crispy, they are deliciously tossed with a choice of tasty sauces. A lentil "kebab" and hearty salad round out the small menu. There's even Greece's only vegan beer. Everything is prepared on the spot, so it takes longer than a classic souvlaki. But the price tag is the same thanks to the owner's commitment to plant-based food without a high price tag. Juicy and with an umami flavor, these gyros are in a league of their own – some may even call them revolutionary.

DEXAMENI

From the Womb to the Tomb

Η Δεξαμενή
Address: Platia Dexameni
(Dexamenis Square),
Kolonaki
Telephone: +30 21 0722 4609
Hours: 10am-2am

The blackboard hanging outside the cramped kitchen reads, "Kindergarten-Bar-Nursing Home," the title jokingly bestowed upon the café by the eminent novelist and poet Alexandros Papadiamantis. He was among the literati who made Dexameni their regular hangout shortly after it opened in the early 1900s – so regular that the place ended up serving as a home-away-from-home for all stages of life. By 2009, however, Dexameni had lost its old-fashioned character, the prices had gone up and the municipality of Athens had begun asking for exorbitant rent, so it closed for a spell. Since reopening in 2012 under the management of two area bar owners, it has been very busy, with locals even queuing up for tables on warm summer nights (reservations are not accepted).

Dexameni is a largely open-air venue. The small stone building houses the kitchen and bathrooms, while tables and chairs are scattered around outside on two wide, steep sidewalks, separated by a pedestrian-only street. Half the fun of eating here is the people-watching.

The menu of meze is varied and offers exceptionally good value for the price. There are the typical Greek mezes and taverna dishes, all made with care: boiled seasonal herbs with lemon, fried smelt, fava bean dip topped with capers and fresh green onions. There are also unusual twists on classics, such as grilled halloumi cheese with fig marmalade and balsamic vinegar, which goes particularly well with ouzo or the light house white. We are also fond of the surprisingly light grilled beef patties with basil and almonds, and the cold salad of brown lentils with sun-dried tomatoes and *manouri* (a white, semi-soft sheep's milk cheese) is ideal on a warm summer night.

This long-treasured café continues to be one of the best places to eat and drink cheaply in downtown Athens. Papadiamantis would feel right at home.

DIPORTO

Time Travel Taverna

Δίπορτο
Address: Sokratous 9 and Theatrou, Downtown
Telephone: +30 210 321 1463
Hours: 8am-7pm; closed Sunday

In business since 1887, Diporto – a defiantly traditional spot in downtown Athens's chaotic market area – has no sign and no menu. The staff doesn't speak a word of English, and you might have to share a table with eccentric old men who look like they stepped out of a folk ballad. From the old-fashioned aluminum wine jugs to the garlic wreaths next to a 1950s fridge and the strong smell of food and smoke that sticks to your clothes, the atmosphere at this basement-level taverna is so reminiscent of the Greece of another era as to be almost eerie, as if by stepping through its doors you have somehow traveled back in time.

Diners don't come to Diporto looking for the latest in culinary experimentation; choices are limited to only five or six dishes each day, based on what's in season and available in the nearby markets. The white-haired owner, Mitsos, a rather brusque athletic figure, lets you know what's on offer. The venue's wintertime specialty – and, to our minds, the highlight of a meal at Diporto – is an excellent chickpea soup that comes in a large, shallow bowl filled to the brim and doused with olive oil; it's enough to feed two people. This is simple home cooking, the chickpeas so soft they almost melt in your mouth. Other dishes, such as Greek salad, a plate of small fried fish, fried sausage or bean soup, are also consistently good.

The house white is a cloudy *retsina* and – as is typical in tavernas – it is ordered by the kilo (a quarter, a half kilo or one kilo) and brought to your table in aluminum wine jugs. Often this is the simplest, cheapest wine available, but when it's good there is something deeply comforting about it, making it the ideal accompaniment to Diporto's home-style cooking.

I KRITI

Cretan Comforts

Η Κρήτη
Address: Veranzerou 5,
            Kanigos Square
Telephone: +30 210 382 6998
Hours: 12:15pm-midnight;
            closed Sunday

There was something about 2006. Food from Crete, one of Greece's largest and most famous islands, was having a moment in Athens (in fact, it still is). Suddenly, Cretan restaurants started popping up all around the city. Traditional Cretan dishes such as the rustic *dakos* (barley rusk in olive oil topped with finely chopped tomato and *mizithra*, a tangy, light, crumbly white cheese) became popular in Greek tavernas.

Unlike those fashionable restaurants, Kriti ("Crete") predates the fad and, more importantly, serves the real thing. Hidden in one of Athens's many arcades, in somewhat drab and hectic Kanigos Square in downtown Athens, Kriti is a shrine to everything Cretan. Cast-iron figures of famous Cretans hang on the walls, while the music that sometimes blares through the speakers is usually that of Nikos Xylouris, the island's most famous singer.

Though they've recently added a printed menu, the owner or his wife or daughter will still come to your table to enumerate the dishes, which are dazzling in both quality and variety. Most people opt for a number of starters, washed down with raki. Our favorites include *stamnagathi* (a spicy wild herb, boiled and best served with lemon), *saganaki* (fried feta in phyllo with honey and sesame seeds), baby tomatoes filled with spicy soft cheese, *xoxlioi* (garlicky snails) and *apaki* (smoked vinegar-marinated pork).

Not to be missed are the delicacies from Sfakia in southwest Crete, such as the local sausage or pita *sfakiani*, a fried pie with mizithra. Dessert – usually dried apricots filled with cream – is on the house.

Service is slow but charmingly so; prepare to spend a minimum of three hours here. Every time you remind Takis, the owner, that you need the bill, he'll serve you another round of raki. Try finding authentic hospitality like that in some of the other "Cretan" joints in town.

TO MAVRO PROVATO

Το Μαύρο Πρόβατο
Address: Arrianou 31, Pagrati
Telephone: +30 210 722 3466
Hours: Mon-Sat, 1pm-midnight;
Sun, 1pm-7pm

Raising the Bar on Meze

To Mavro Provato ("The Black Sheep") once advertised itself as a *mezedopoleio,* a place that does mezes. In reality, the only thing about it that will remind you of a typical mezedopoleio – often stereotyped as a cheap hangout place that is not necessarily high in quality – is the prices. The value for money, combined with a lovely environment and great attention to detail, keeps Mavro Provato busy at all times of day. Reservations are a must.

The menu is divided into three sections: salads, cold dishes and warm dishes. The fresh and crispy salad with *katiki Domokou* cheese – a soft, light goat cheese – is a definite winner. The combination of barley rusks, spinach and finely chopped tomato in this salad makes for a crunchy texture, in direct antithesis to the creaminess of the tangy cheese. The wide range of warm dishes includes the unusual meatballs with ouzo and mint, as well as pancetta, which is marinated here in fresh herbs and pepper, the latter giving it a sweet edge. Also particularly strong are the meat dishes, including a spicy, heavy and wintry beef sausage that is a rare delicacy from the city of Drama in Northern Greece; it's an excellent meze for ouzo. The *hunkar begenti,* a Turkish dish popular in Athens, is also a standout, the beef (rather than lamb) stewed in tomato sauce and served with a smooth eggplant purée.

One of the advantages of Mavro Provato's being a "mezedopoleio" is that it offers the opportunity to try a variety of liqueurs and drinks rarely found in mainstream restaurants. In addition to tsipouro (a strong white spirit produced from wine-press residue, akin to grappa), there are five different ouzo brands on offer (we recommend the well-trusted Pitsiladi brand from Mytilene, aka Lesbos) as well as raki (unlike the Turkish version, this strong spirit has no aniseed flavor). But our personal favorite is the *rakomelo,* warm tsipouro or raki mixed with honey and spices.

AROUND THE ACROPOLIS

CAFÉ AVISSINIA

Flea Market Find

Καφέ Αβυσσηνία
Address: Kinetou 7, Plateia
         Avissinias, Monastiraki
Telephone: +30 210 321 7047
Hours: Tues, Thurs-Sun, 1pm-1am;
       Wed, 6pm-1am

Sooner or later, almost everyone in Athens, tourist or local, heads for the flea market, the city's oldest bazaar, below Monastiraki Square. Although it's busiest on Sundays, all week long you can rummage through the antiques spread out in colorful disorder in front of the small shops that line all four sides of Avissinia Square.

One treasure that requires neither a keen eye nor a connoisseur's expertise is Café Avissinia, the square's only establishment where the antiques are not for sale. A restaurant/watering hole where you can stop for a coffee or a full-course meal, the café is more than just a place to grab a bite. With its old-fashioned rush-seated chairs, marble-topped tables and pink floral wallpaper, it feels part ancestral home, part elegant 19th-century Viennese coffeehouse – that is, if a Vienese coffeehouse could also have a terrace with Acropolis views.

That the café blends in perfectly with the square was no accident. Its owner-founder, Ketty Koufonikola, chose the location because it reflected her own interest in art and antiques. And because it seemed like a good place where she could combine them with her other passions, cooking and entertaining.

As her son and current manager, Nikolas, told us, when she opened the café in 1986, the upstairs still operated as an auction house, and the all-male proprietors of the antiques shops did not take kindly to this female interloper. "Acceptance came in 1989, when a fire broke out in the square. Ketty remained in her kitchen all night, cooking onion soup for the shop owners, and after that they took her into their hearts. She was no longer an outsider," he said.

The menu has always reflected Ketty's background, with dishes from Macedonia – her parents were prosperous landowners from Kozani – and Cyprus, where her husband's family originated, with additions

from her own culinary experiences in international London, and even a few ideas from faithful clientele.

Though the menu changes with the seasons, some offerings are permanent, such as George's eggs (baked with sausage and tomato) and couscous with vegetables and homemade chutney, a recipe from a Greek customer from Ethiopia. Some of our favorites include the grilled eel, marinated *gavros* (anchovies), oven-baked eggplant, baked mushrooms, pork with leeks and prunes (a very Macedonian combination), *koupepia* (Cypriot-style vine leaves) and octopus salad. And of course, as we said, this is not just a place to grab a bite or even linger over a beautifully presented, tasty meal. On weekend evenings and Sunday afternoons, Café Avissinia turns into a musical fiesta. Definitely the best find in this flea market.

FABRIKA TOU EFROSINOU

Η Φάμπρικα του Ευρόσυνου
Address: An. Zinni 34, Koukaki
Telephone: +30 210 924 6354
Hours: Tues-Fri, 5pm-11pm;
       Sat, 1pm-midnight;
       Sun, 5pm-11pm

Blessed Kitchen

In the once-quiet central Athens district of Koukaki, now the talk of the town among food lovers and night owls, Fabrika tou Efrosinou immediately captures one's attention with its clever name: Fabrika, factory in Russian, has the same meaning in Greek slang, usually with communist connotations; Efrosinos is the Greek Orthodox patron saint of all cooks.

Co-owner Giorgos Gatsos is the restaurant's chef and seems to have been blessed by Saint Efrosinos himself. From his father, a fisherman, he learned to appreciate simple cooking using few but high-quality ingredients. He studied theology in Belgrade and spent time in Greek monasteries, where he was trained in monastery-style cooking, a healthy traditional cuisine focusing primarily on fresh seasonal vegetables and legumes, artisanal cheeses and yogurt, sourdough bread, olive oil and wine. His partner, Athina Tsoli, is an accomplished winemaker with a passion for good food. Unsurprisingly, the wine list here is top notch.

Portions are generous, and we recommend ordering a few dishes to share. We thoroughly enjoyed a beautiful carrot salad with almonds and chopped rose *loukoumi* (the Greek version of Turkish delight). We also ordered the savory pumpkin pie with goat-milk feta and the meat pie, both delicious. The grilled *manouri* (a white, semi-soft, mild, creamy cheese made from goat or sheep's milk, with a subtle nutty flavor) was perfectly complemented by an olive marmalade and sesame seeds. The fish *pastourma* (cured, smoked cod fillet with fenugreek and sea salt) was also excellent. If available, *isli kefte*, cracked wheat patties stuffed with minced meat and pine nuts, are a must-try, and we loved the *sarmadakia,* bite-sized dolma with rice and herbs served with yogurt. As a main we had the slow-roasted rooster, served with hand-made Greek-style noodles, and for dessert a carob tart with orange cream and a yogurt mousse with lemon zest, a lovely ending to this delightful meal.

FATSIO

Address: Eufroniou 5, Pagrati
Telephone: +30 210 7217421
Hours: 11am-6pm

A Taste of Old Constantinople

The brown wooden door at Fatsio looks like the entry to an old house. Inside are velvet curtains, old family photos, tables set properly with well-ironed white linens and vintage dinnerware with their logo, Fatsio, printed on each plate. Everything is well-preserved and the place holds an old-school finesse and elegance that is rare to find these days in an affordable lunch spot like this. What can also be found inside is a living link to another time and place, that of Istanbul when the city still had a sizable Greek community.

The food served at Fatsio is referred to as *Politiki kouzina,* meaning "cuisine from the city" – a style of cooking with Byzantine-Greek and Ottoman hints all beautifully blended together, which was developed by what used to be a thriving Greek community in Constantinople (present-day Istanbul). This is from where the Fatsio family hails. They arrived in Athens in 1964, when rising political tensions led to the large-scale departure of Greeks from Turkey. Having shuttered their two restaurants on Istanbul's Prince's Islands, patriarch Constantinos eventually opened Fatsio Athens in 1969.

The leather-clad menu cover hasn't changed at all through the years, nor have the recipes inside. Classic old-school starters such as cocktail prawns, *taramosalata* (fish roe salad) and octopus in vinegar are always available, as is a long list of salads. To follow, the slow-cooked dishes of seasonal vegetables with olive oil known as *mageirefta* are what Fatsio is particularly well known for. Among their most famous are the artichokes *a la Polita,* which are braised in olive oil and lemon juice along with potatoes and carrots, the stuffed zucchini with minced meat dressed in a light tomato sauce, and the eggplant pouches filled with chopped veal. Apart from the daily dishes which are usually popular and sell out pretty early, Fatsio also does several dishes "a la minute," mostly grilled

meats and fish. Two options of old-school desserts are available daily, all of which evoke sweet childhood memories.

The restaurant is most busy on weekends, and especially Sundays, when the family prepares even more daily dishes in order to please old customers – many of them with family roots in Istanbul – who drive in from the suburbs to eat there and be reminded of a time now long gone.

JOSHUA TREE

Address: Anapafseos 13, Mets
Telephone: +30 210 9239747
Hours: 8am-midnight

Where Coffee and Vegan Lovers Unite

Each year, Greek coffee drinkers become more sophisticated in their tastes, and it's not uncommon to hear requests for a certain coffee blend or roast, almond milk (or other nut milks) in place of regular milk, or even high-quality ice that doesn't melt as fast. This new and intense interest in quality coffee could explain why Joshua Tree Café opening just as the Covid lockdowns started wasn't a death sentence. Defying all expectations, it quickly became a hit spot.

Just behind Kallimarmaron, the marble Panathenaic Stadium, is the oft-unexplored neighborhood of Mets, where the hip and funky coffee shop has drawn a dedicated young crowd. (Though, thankfully, they're the kind that thrive on relaxed, friendly vibes.) At Joshua Tree, you can choose between coffee from Brazil, Ethiopia or Papua New Guinea, as well as various nut milks on offer. What we particularly love is their blend of coconut and oat milk, which creams wonderfully. It adds a natural sweetness and beautiful aroma to the coffee. We like to pair our *freddo* (shaken espresso over ice) with one of their sensational miso cookies or another of their tasty vegan/vegetarian snacks, which are baked daily in house. From "cheese"cakes to tarts to cinnamon rolls, there's no need to down your coffee solo. There is also a wide range of lattes, ranging from the classic, to matcha, to creative riffs that include ingredients like beetroot and blue algae.

Another thing we love: Vegetarian or vegan brunch is served almost all day, with great smoothies and smoothie bowls, egg dishes, vegan burgers and more. Particularly noteworthy are the cocktails that are swung out in the evenings, as well as the selection of Greek natural wines that can be paired with healthy nibbles.

PARKBENCH

Address: Pramanton 10, Koukaki
Telephone: +30 2121065303
Hours: 1:30pm-11:45pm

The Best Seat in Athens

All ages meet in the *platia* (plaza) of Greek neighborhoods: babies in strollers, loud children running and playing like there's no tomorrow, teenagers having their first smoke or kiss. These squares are to be found all around the country, even in the most remote village. In the backstreets of Athens's Koukaki neighborhood lies a special plaza that is a bit greener and larger than others – you could even call it a small park. Apart from the many benches in Elpida (ελπίδα, meaning hope), there are tables and chairs belonging to the cute little restaurant across the street. Here, ParkBench was opened in August 2018 by couple Dimitris Soutsos and Aspa Selepe and their friend Stelios (who left the endeavor in 2020).

ParkBench is relaxed and simple, with a clean, minimal design and a few retro hints here and there. The kitchen is open, and inside are a few tables for rainy days. But thanks to Athens's typically ideal weather, the large outdoor space – both on the sidewalk right outside and across the street in the plaza – makes for ample seating. Their menu has hints of Asian and Mediterranean cuisines, with a long list of traditional Greek ingredients. For instance, the classic *kolokythokeftedes* – the zucchini fritters found on most Greek taverna menus and typically served with yogurt or tzatziki – are here paired with a light and pleasantly tangy cashew cream, made with chile and lime.

More unexpected are the sushi platters with a Greek twist and a bright pink seafood linguini with beet pesto (their bestseller). For dessert, the thyme gelato is divine. Due to its location and because the plaza at certain hours of the day attracts families and children, they also offer a simpler kids menu with smaller portions and lower prices. Finally, their wine list is superb. It's designed by All About Wine, a team of experts in Athens who promote Greek wines,

especially those made by small producers. The rest is left to what's in season, the team's creativity and available ingredients.

Before snagging your seat at ParkBench, just be sure of one thing: You get there when there's still light out. Soak in the Greek plaza vibe with a plate of great food and a glass of perfect wine.

SEYCHELLES

Post-Industrial Cooking

Σεϋχέλλες
Address: Keramikou 49, Metaxourge
Telephone +30 211 183 4789
(reservations recommended)
Hours: 1:30pm-2am

The best *mezedopoleio* in Athens,s Seychelles is located in a revitalized former industrial zone, and it's jam-packed every single night. Young owners Anna and Fotis clearly love what they do and work hard to keep standards high with their creative, seasonal, ever-changing menu that blends the traditional and modern and focuses on using ingredients made by small producers from around Greece.

Daytime at Seychelles is for enjoying a cup of coffee or the famous ginger juice at the bar. Lunch starts at 1:30 p.m., and the kitchen serves food continuously until late. The atmosphere is always friendly and casual, and the wait staff maintains its efficiency and good humor even when the place gets extremely busy.

The daily specials are full of surprises, all worth trying. We like the chickpea salad with fresh mint and feta cheese, octopus cooked in red wine and served on creamed peas, beef tongue grilled to perfection, and vegetable-stuffed beets served with yogurt. For a very traditional option, there's *sougania*, a Lesbos recipe for onions stuffed with cracked wheat, fresh herbs and oxtail and sprinkled with chili flakes. The sweet and spicy pork cutlets are also popular, and we would be hard-pressed to not order the braised beef cheeks served on crispy hand-cut fried potatoes when they're available.

The cheese list benefits from Fotis's unimpeachable sourcing. Besides excellent traditional cheeses from all over the country, there's a selection of cured fish, such as smoked swordfish and tuna from Kalymnos island, smoked sardines and salt cod.

The wide range of *tsipouro, raki,* Greek beer and wines complements the thoughtfully composed and well-executed menu. Most plates are priced at an excellent value, particularly because these are dishes meant for sharing, but also because Seychelles is one of the best places in town to experience a real Athenian night out.

BEYOND THE CENTER

ARGOURA

Seafood Surprise

Άργουρα
Address: Agisilaou 49-51, Tzitzifies
Telephone +30 217 717 3200
Hours: 7:30pm-midnight,
        closed Sundays

On the outside, Argoura looks like just another neighborhood tavern, but the nets in the covered courtyard hint at what the kitchen's up to: fresh seafood with a flavorful twist.

Owner and chef Nikos Michail puts so much effort and love in what he offers, carefully selecting every single ingredient himself daily. The restaurant is named after his village on the island of Evia, which is where most of the fish and seafood he serves comes from. Frying is out of question here – Michail prefers cooking methods that highlight the freshness of his ingredients.

He welcomes guests with a complimentary fish soup, and we recommend following that up with the green salad with sea urchin dressing and the *taramosalata* (fish roe dip) with sweet potato. Among his signature dishes is undoubtedly the marinated (uncooked, ceviche-style) seafood, pristinely fresh and bracingly flavorful: elegant white sea bream infused with bergamot and tuna with sweet vinegar. The smoked eel served with an eggplant purée is a must, and so is the handmade *goglies* (traditional gnocchi-like pasta from Evia) with langoustines. The menu is full of other surprises too, including mussels with seaweed and lemon sauce, and prawns with fava beans.

We recommend ending your meal with a sweet *bougatsa*, layers of phyllo with a pumpkin custard sprinkled with generous amounts of cinnamon, and a shot of the dried-fruit infused *tsipouro*.

BASE GRILL

The Meat Is On

Address: Leoforos
Konstantinoupoleos 64,
Peristeri
Telephone: +30 210 575 7455
Hours: 1pm-12:15am

Twin brothers Spiros and Vangelis Liakos have taken the art of grilling to new heights at their steakhouse, located near bustling Bournazi Square in Athens's western suburbs. Base Grill has the atmosphere of a modern tavern: old posters on the walls, soft colors, nothing extravagant. The space is often packed, so we recommend reserving – especially on weekends.

The menu consists of hearty portions of pork chops, rib eye, Brazilian-style cuts served on wooden plates, beef liver, sausages made from heritage-breed pigs and burgers, as well as their accompaniments.

Each cut of meat is grilled with its own specific technique. When it's done, the waiter brings it to the table and skillfully cuts it into thin slices. Our carefully aged sirloin, cooked medium-rare, arrived at the table escorted by classic sea salt, citrus salt and smoked salt with cedar. We ordered the *picania* – a deeply flavorful and juicy rump cut – well done, so the cooks first cut it into filets and then grilled the pieces to ensure that it would still be supremely tender.

Base Grill also makes excellent salads, but our favorite non-meat dish is the "sunny-side up eggs with potatoes." At the table, the waiter breaks the runny yolks with a spoon and spreads them on the nest of hot fried potato – so simple and so delicious.

The beverage list is inspired. Wines are categorized according to provenance (Attica, Central Greece, Peloponnese, Santorini, Macedonia, Thessaly), and the house red is respectable, while beer is also given its due, with selections from a number of Greek artisanal brewers.

The bill arrived with treats: frozen mastic liqueur, a pleasant *digestif*, and a small éclair for each diner. It's that attention to detail – and no doubt the lingering good feeling from a generous send-off – that makes Base Grill a favorite for many a meat lover.

CHARA

Χαρά
Address: Patission 339
Telephone: +30 210 228 7266
Hours: 9:30am-midnight

Just Like in the Movies

Patission Avenue, officially called 28is Oktovriou, connects the once-grand, now down-at-heel neighborhoods of Patissia and Kypseli to Omonia Square. It's home to some of Athens's most important landmarks. Χαρά (pronounced "Chara") sits at the end of it, by the Ano Patissia suburban railway station.

The original owner, Chara, came from Istanbul and apparently carried the recipe for *ekmek kadayıfı* (bread pudding) and *kaymak* (clotted cream) in her shoe. She opened the dessert shop in 1969, and her family still owns the place, which looks like it's stuck firmly in the '80s, with its sepia glass walls, old-fashioned logo and an enormous brown catalog of decadent sweets that are fanciful in name and presentation. The shop started out offering "Istanbul-style" desserts but made its name selling two things: ekmek topped with kaymak ice cream and a wonderful ice cream concoction called Chicago.

Where Greek ekmek usually tops *kataifi* (shredded phyllo) with whipped cream and nuts, Chara's ekmek is closer to the Turkish version: the bottom is essentially a bread pudding drenched in syrup and then topped with kaymak, a luscious clotted cream made from buffalo's milk. The shop offers six versions of ekmek, the most popular of which is the one topped with *kaimaki* (the Greek name for kaymak) ice cream. The base is almost chewy with sweet syrup and is complemented perfectly by the rich, slippery ice cream. It's a masterpiece, and a rather pricey dessert by Athenian standards.

The Chicago is a nostalgic classic loved by children, combining chocolate ice cream with whipped cream, chocolate sauce and chopped almonds. It's a chocoholic's dream – and is even better when the ice cream begins to melt and pools into the chocolate sauce.

Patission Avenue's best days are now behind it, but decades on, Chara's still going strong.

KOSMIKON

King of Galaktoboureko

Ζαχαροπλαστείο Κοσμικόν
Αγ.Νικόλαος
Address: Ionias 104, Agios Nikolaos
Telephone: +30 210 864 9124
Hours: 7am-11pm

Ζαχαροπλαστείο Κοσμικόν
Αγ.Ελευθέριος
Address: Chrysostomou Smyrnis 69,
Agios Eleftherios
Telephone: +30 210 202 3350
Hours: 7am-11pm

When invited to dinner or coffee at a friend's house, Greeks often arrive bearing big, rectangular patisserie boxes containing anything from a large cheesecake to ice cream- and sorbet-layered cakes. But more often than not, these boxes contain a pan of the Greek national dessert, galaktoboureko.

The Greek version of the syrupy phyllo desserts popular all over the Middle East, galaktoboureko (gala means "milk," börek is the Turkish word for filled pastries) is a custard pie that sandwiches a cream made with milk, eggs and semolina flour between layers of thin phyllo, and the whole thing is doused in syrup. This pie remains a firm local favorite, and Kosmikon is the undisputed king of Athenian galaktoboureko.

An old-fashioned dessert shop operating since 1961, it now has five locations around Athens. The galaktoboureko here is done the traditional way, with butter from Thessaly in central Greece or Mytilene, homemade phyllo and – most importantly – no lemon or orange flavoring, just the traditional vanilla.

The result is that rare thing when it comes to phyllo-based, syrup-drenched desserts: a wonderfully balanced concoction, sweet but not too sweet, with cream oozing from the sides, and the phyllo remaining thin and crisp.

We recommend going to the two central locations in Agios Nikolaos and Agios Eleftherios for their charmingly retro atmosphere.

OUZERI TOU LAKI

Landlocked Seaside Oasis

Ουζερί του Λάκη
Address: 16 Elpidos Street, Victoria
Square
Telephone: +30 210 8213776
Hours: Mon-Sat, noon-1am;
Sun, noon-6pm

On the cool March day we entered Ouzeri tou Laki, the taverna didn't look particularly inviting. We had on good word that it was worth the stop, however, and stepping into the simple room was like stepping into any classic fish place on the Aegean coast. To one's right is a display case brimming with bright-eyed fish of many types and sizes, while nautical motifs prevail on the pale blue walls. Moreover, one wall is papered with clippings of rave reviews from Greek and international papers, including The New York Times. It appears as if the taverna is a common secret.

Giorgos, who tends the till, tells us that Lakis Lambrou was his father and he'd had a shop selling automobile spare parts, batteries and spark plugs, until he had the unlikely idea to open a fish restaurant in the heart of Athens in 1984. Lakis has since passed on, but Giorgos and his wife, Anna, haven't changed anything. The menu depends on the catch of the day, which arrives from Kymi on the east coast of Evia and Skyros, opposite it, by noon. Apart from whatever fresh fish beckon from their icy bed, you can choose from a wide range of salads and mezedes, to unusual creations from Lakis himself (like the sardine moussaka). To satisfy as many of our urges as possible, we chose a fixed price combo that included a platter of boiled greens, fried baby squid, anchovies sofrito, chickpea fritters, and potato salad with anchovies (known as mezes tou Laki). Each dish was delectable but the portions were so generous that half of the meal came home with us. Now, whenever we have a craving for the sea and are unable to get there, here is where we return – and we quickly did so just one month later.

The house white is more than pleasant, beer drinkers will find two Greek microbreweries among the better-known big names, and there are 16 brands of ouzo to choose from. More important, Giorgos and

Anna are so warm and welcoming that after just two visits, we felt like old friends (and so, we observed, did the rest of the clientele, who all seemed to be regulars). And on a warm summer evening, you can sit at tables outside on the sidewalk, for Elpidos Street has no cars to bother you. There won't be a sea breeze, but that will be all that's missing.

TOMAS KEBAB

As the Kosmos Turns

Τόμας Κεμπάπ
Address: Mitrou Sarkoudinou 49,
Neos Kosmos
Telephone: +30 210 901 5981,
+30 210 901 9328
Hours: 11am-12:30am,
closed Sundays

Hampartsoum Tomasian – known to all as Tomas – sits on the doorstep of his kebab joint in Neos Kosmos, greeting passersby in Greek, Armenian and Arabic. Tomas is part of a second wave of Armenian migration to this neighborhood; he grew up in Syria and Lebanon but can trace his origins back to Diyarbakır, a city in southeastern Turkey.

Tomas, 56, worked for a fellow Armenian at a souvlaki joint in Monastiraki Square before striking out on his own. Soon people from all over Athens were flocking to Neos Kosmos to taste one of the best kebabs in town.

We asked Tomas what makes his kebabs so special. "There is no secret ingredient," he said. "I only add top-quality minced lamb and veal, salt and chopped onion. I brought a machine from Syria that chops onion to the size of a rice grain – that's what makes my kebabs extra moist." He also makes *içli köfte* (fried bulgur-crusted meatballs), falafel, baba ghanoush, hummus, *yoğurtlu kebap* (kebab with yogurt sauce) and *lahmacun* (crisp, oven-baked flatbread covered with minced meat and herbs). Tomas's silky, savory kebabs are garnished simply with onions and tomatoes, thankfully undiluted by tzatziki or French fries.

Originally a shantytown, Neos Kosmos sprung up to house the thousands of Anatolian Christians who had fled from Asia Minor after the Greco-Turkish War. These Anatolian Greeks and Armenians have now been well integrated into Greek society and have left Neos Kosmos behind to settle in more upscale neighborhoods. But the new Middle Eastern immigrants since the early 1990s are bringing it back to life.

Tomas may be one of these newcomers, but he is part and parcel of this neighborhood's busy history, sharing tales of the urban landscape – how it evolved during the decades, the socioeconomic changes that had taken place in the area and the vanished memories of the old residents. Tomas is proud of a past that was never his own, remembering what many Athenians either forget or ignore.

TO RODI

From Armenia, with Souvlaki

Κεμπάπ Το Ρόδι
Address: 163 Kreontos and 179 Rodou, Sepolia
Telephone: +30 210 515 4376 or +30 210 512 7444
Hours: 11am-1am

Over the past few decades, the working-class suburb of Sepolia in western Athens has developed rapidly and is now full of high-rise apartment buildings. Though it still has a neighborhood feel, there aren't many dining venues, which makes To Rodi – an Armenian restaurant and souvlaki joint that makes some of the best kebabs in Athens – seem particularly incongruous.

To Rodi – Greek for "The Pomegranate," one of the national fruits of Armenia – opened in 2000 under the name Agop Kebab and moved to its current location a few years before the Covid-19 pandemic. The place is always buzzing: large families and other groups of locals crowd around the tables under the harsh neon lights, while delivery boys come and go. Some of the friendly staff are members of the Zatikian family, who own the place.

The extensive menu consists of a mix of classic Armenian dishes and traditional Greek souvlaki fare. The wonderful *lahmacun*, flatbread topped with ground meat, tomatoes, peppers and onions and resembling a thin, spicy pizza, makes for a light treat. Another unusual taste – even for Greeks – are the eggplant rolls stuffed with crushed walnuts, tomato and bulgur and topped with pomegranate seeds. This heavy, spicy dish is dominated by the flavor of the walnuts. We also tried the juicy *khinkali*, a type of Georgian dumpling, similar to Armenian and Turkish *mantı*, which is stuffed with a tasty mixture of ground beef, lamb, garlic and dill.

One cannot leave To Rodi without trying its specialty, kebabs. There are four different versions, shish kebab, yogurt kebab, Adana kebab and Iskender kebab. We are fans of the second. The spicy, succulent meat is served with a tangy yogurt sauce atop freshly chopped pita – a messy but delicious combination that seems like the perfect symbol of the cultural and culinary mashup that is To Rodi.

VARSOS

Βάρσος Κηφισιάς
Address: Kassaveti 5, Kifisia
Telephone: +30 210 801 2472
Hours: 7am-midnight

Nostalgia, with Cream on Top

A visit to Varsos is like traveling back in time to one of the city's grand patisseries of the 1950s. The venue, which has always been in the hands of the Varsos family, is one of the most famous of Athens's old-style coffee houses and is the only one that has kept its traditional charm over the last several decades.

Varsos was established in 1892 in central Athens, but it is the wonderfully old-fashioned Kifisia location, to which the patisserie moved in 1932, that has made the venue famous. With its decorative high ceilings and beautiful mosaic floors framed with pink marble, the interior feels nothing less than grand.

The patisserie serves all the old-style Greek desserts anyone could wish for, but it is best known for three specialties. The first is pure, fresh whipped cream. An entire fridge is dedicated to holding plastic jars of the stuff, which is rich and pleasantly fatty but not sweet and, as any good housewife from Athens's northern suburbs can testify, never, ever runny. The second specialty is the meringues, which are the best in Athens. Sold in a dizzying array of shapes and sizes, these airy beauties melt in your mouth.

But our favorite – and the favorite of an entire generation of Athenians who grew up on this recipe – is the *tsoureki*, a sweet, eggy, golden-hued bread similar to brioche. The dough is also used to make a version of croissant. The *gemisto* ("filled") croissant, a sort of rectangular tsoureki with chocolate, walnuts and brown sugar, can almost bring tears to the eyes of those who were raised on Varsos products.

The patisserie's marathon operating hours are a testament to its ability to pull in a steady stream of customers. For Athenians, it seems, any time is the right time for a little culinary time travel.

PIRAEUS AND THE DOCKS

MARGARO

Pillar of Piraeus

Μαργαρώ
Address: Leoforos Chatzikyriakou 12
Piraeus
Telephone: +30 2104514226
Hours: Mon-Sat, noon-midnight,
Sun, noon-5:30pm

Piraeus, located about 10 kilometers south of downtown Athens, is not just the largest port of Greece, but it is also among the top five most-important ports in Europe. Aside from the port, Piraeus covers a large area, some of which is residential and other parts which are more industrial. Though it may seem chaotic at first glance – especially for the many visitors who arrive at the port by ferry from a lovely little island and are shocked to suddenly find themselves in a gray city – the truth is that Piraeus hides a nostalgic flair and charm that is rare to come across in cities these days.

Due to the fact that Piraeus is the main link between Athens and many of the nearby islands, it has historically been inhabited by islanders, sailors and seamen. Margaro, short for Margarita, was one of the islanders that moved from Mykonos to Piraeus in the early 20th century. In 1917, young Margaro opened her first *oinopoleion,* an old-school term used for an eatery that sells wine, expanding and moving shop multiple items. Eventually, her son, Lazaros, dubbed their taverna Margaro in 1970, turning it into one of the most historic places to eat in the whole of Attica – a true cult favorite.

Hidden in a corner right by the Greek Naval Academy, the location is unique. When the weather is good, the restaurant scatters tables out in the street. From there, watch young cadets dressed in sparkling white uniforms entering and exiting their school.

The menu is small (in fact, there's no written version) and that's its main charm: specials include *koutsomoura* (a local type of red mullet), fried shrimp and scampi (when in season) and, occasionally, fried pandora (a white fish in the sea bream family) if they come across it fresh. The fish, all fried on a two-burner stove, are served with fresh bread and Margaro's famous tomato salad. And that's about it – all of Margaro's regulars already know their order!

TAXIDEVONTAS

Fisherman's Friend

Ταξιδεύοντας
Address: Platonos 72, Piraeus
Telephone: +30 210 432 4368
Web: www.taxidevontas.com
Hours: 1pm-midnight

In Piraeus, there is a tacit agreement among locals to keep treasured taverns and restaurants hidden, lest they be overrun by the tourists arriving on the cruise ships that dock in town. This is particularly true of Keratsini, a neighborhood on the outskirts of the port city.

One of the "hidden" places where Keratsini locals like to gather is Taxidevontas, located near the Anastasi Cemetery. Owners Kostas Zafeiropoulos and Yannis Zois are longtime amateur fishermen, and over the years they had become friends with many boat captains and other fishermen all over Greece. Realizing that they already had the kind of seafood purveyors that other restaurateurs would kill for, they opened Taxidevontas in 2002, in the neighborhood where they were born and raised and continue to live, bringing their relatives on board to work as staff. Those fishermen friends now show up daily – even during dinnertime, their fresh catch in tow.

This includes an intriguing variety of impeccably fresh seafood: mussels, shrimp, lobster and squid, as well as mackerel that the restaurant smokes in-house, tuna, and other fish big and small that you can have fried or grilled to order. Zafeiropoulos and Zois are always on the lookout for unusual specimens, such as ray, the cartilaginous fish that is related to skate, to put on the daily changing menu, even if there's enough just for one or two lucky diners.

Our favorite preparation is the fish soup, which comes to the table in a beautiful tureen. The broth is deeply saturated with the rich, pure flavors of the sea and is accompanied by a platter of boiled red fish and chunks of carrot, potato and zucchini – humble ingredients, the sum of which is so much greater than the parts. We often end our meals of grilled sardines and shellfish salad with a shot of mastic liqueur and a platter of sweets: Greek yogurt with homemade jam and orange and walnut pie. Based on that final course, it's clear Zafeiropoulos and Zois have the right friends in other places, too.

TO EIDIKON

Extra Special

Το Ειδικόν
Address: Psaron 38 & Salaminos,
Piraeus
Telephone: +30 210 461 2674
Hours: 11am-11:30pm,
closed Sundays

At the corner of Psaron and Salaminos streets, in a quiet neighborhood of Piraeus, there's a place that looks straight out of a 1960s Greek black-and-white movie. Its name, *eidikon,* means "special," and it's the last of its kind: a *bakalotaverna,* or grocery store and eatery, all in one.

The interior, with its dark wooden paneling, was obviously built to last. The shelves and old refrigerator cases are covered with vintage '60s products, bric-a-brac and photographs of owner Apostolos Papakonstantinou and his forebears, who opened the shop in 1920. On Saturday evenings, there is live music, and the place stays open later, but if you're lucky, you might witness one of the spontaneous parties where everyone joins in, eating, drinking and making merry.

On a recent visit, Apostolos – everyone knows him by his first name – brought us a jug of his retsina wine and a few of the dishes they make fresh daily: fried calf's liver, meatballs, tomato salad (with three types of olives), a firm DOP cheese from Amfilochia and "the cake," fries topped with four eggs sunny-side up. The rest of the menu continues in the same vein: *soutzouki* (spicy salami/ sausage) either fried or raw, feta cheese, fava (split pea puree) and omelettes. The one made with corned beef is a customer favorite.

The meatballs were fluffy and had a hint of mint and garlic, the potatoes were expertly fried in olive oil, and the liver was soft and delicate. We were pleasantly surprised by the retsina; the home-made variety tend to be oxidized and not very good, but this one was still fresh, with just a hint of resin. Besides wine, there's also beer, *ouzo* and *tsipouro.*

Our meal ended with humble tahini halva on the house. This type of halva is known as *tou bakali* (grocer's halva), because it was always bought from the store and never made at home. Another welcome throwback is the prices, which are happily stuck in the 1980s.

«Η ΣΤΡΟΦΗ» ΚΟΥΤΡΟ... ΞΟΞΙΝΟΣΗ

ΓΑΥΡΟΣ	ΧΑΛΑΝΑΡΙ ΡΟΔΕΛΑ	ΓΑΡΙΔΑΚΙ ΦΡΕ
ΜΑΡΙΔΑΚΙ	»	ΒΑΡΑΒΛΑΚΙ »
ΚΟΤΣΟΜΟΥΡΑΛΙ »	ΓΟΝΟΣ	ΧΤΑΠΟΔΙ ΦΗ
ΘΕΡΙΝΑ	ΚΑΒΟΥΡΙ	» ΞΥΔΑ
ΜΠΑΚΑΛΙΑΡΑΚΙΑ	ΜΠΑΚΑΛΙΑΡΟΣ	ΜΥΔΙΑ
ΣΟΥΠΙΑ ΦΡΕΣ	ΓΑΛΕΟΣ	ΧΑΛΑΟΝΙΑ
ΑΡΓΑΝΕΣ	ΓΑΡΙΔΕΣ Νο1	ΑΧΙΝΟΣ
ΡΑΒΑΙΑ	» Νο3	ΠΕΡΚΑ/ΛΗ
ΙΕΡΙΝΙΑ	ΣΟΥΠΙΑ ΦΡ	ΠΟΡΦΥΡΕΣ
ΛΥΚΑΝΙΚΟ	ΜΥΔΟΠΙΛΑΦΟ	ΤΥΡΟΚΡΟΚΕ
ΣΑΝΙΑ	ΦΑΒΑ	ΤΥΡΟΠΙΤΑ
ΡΙΖΟΛΕΣ ΧΟΙΡ.	ΣΑΓΑΝΑΚΙ ΤΥΡΙ	ΦΛΟΓΕΡΕ
ΑΥΓΑ ΤΗΓΑΝ.		» ΛΑΧΑ

ΠΑΤΑΤΑ	ΧΟΡΙΑΤΙΚΗ	
	ΜΑΡΟΥΛΙ	
ΟΣΑΛΑΤΑ	ΛΑΧΑΝΟ.	ΓΡΑΒΙΕ
ΣΑΛΑΤΑ	ΠΑΝΤΖΑΡΙΑ	ΡΟΚΦΟ
ΑΥΓΟΛΕΜ	ΧΟΡΤΑ (ΒΛΙΤΑ)	ΦΕ

SPECIALS

ATHENS UNCORKED

New Wave Greek Wine and Retsina

In antiquity, Greek wine was exported across the Mediterranean, yet in the modern era, it has never gotten much of a foothold on the international market. These days though, we're seeing an enological renaissance as young winemakers experiment with single-vineyard wines and dig into terroir, special blends and even sparkling wines. A new crop of wine bars have opened in Athens that give both locals and visitors the chance to taste some great domestic varieties — including a lighter, more refreshing style of retsina, a sweet wine infused with pine resin that's historically gotten a bad rap.

Oinoscent was the first wine bar that opened in downtown Athens, and is still very popular with young professionals. The atmosphere is smart yet casual, with aluminum chairs and warm décor. Oinoscent's well-trained staff are happy to offer informed advice in English about what to choose from the wine list. The food is also excellent to pair with your wonderful wines. If you want to try one of the new-wave retsinas, we recommend Tear of the Pine, Se Fonto Rose – a rosé retsina – and Ritinitis Nobilis.

Located just off Ermou, Athens's biggest commercial street, **Heteroclito** is one of our favorite Athens wine bars in terms of location and décor: The downstairs area is like a nonsmoking French bistro, while the upstairs is an ode to the '60s and '70s in Athens, with mosaic floors and Danish furniture. The emphasis here is on Greek wine and Greek grape varieties. Indeed, all of the wines served by the glass are Greek. We love the malagousia, a delicate, aromatic white grape with citrusy and stone fruit notes from northern Greece. The award-winning Samos Nectar, a rich, sweet dessert wine, is also worthy of note.

Located in one of the Syntagma area's most beautiful arcades, **By the Glass** offers an interesting twist. Customers can pick and choose what

they want to try and in what quantity, with pours offered as 25, 75 or 150 ml. There are about 90 labels available, of which 19 are offered by the glass, making the venue a great place to taste different varieties. The venue attracts a somewhat older and more mature clientele.

Newcomer **Junior Does Wine** is another spot we love, owing to the pleasant vibes and outdoor seating by the small park across the street. The excellent menu and budget-friendly wine list attracts a rather young crowd.

Materia Prima has two branches in downtown Athens, the first one in Pagrati and the second in Koukaki. Both are tiny, with only a few tables indoors and the rest outdoors. Apart

from being one of the finest wine bars here in Athens, they also serve delicious dishes to pair. Even more, they have both an online and physical wine store (at the Pagrati branch). Their well-trained sommeliers will happily introduce you to the world of Greek wines. Ask for their biodynamic wine options as well as the natural wines on offer.

By the Glass
Address: Georgiou Souri 3, Syntagma
Telephone: +30 210 323 2560
Hours: 1pm-2am

Heteroclito
Address: Fokionos 2, Syntagma
Telephone: +30 210 323 9406
Hours: Mon-Thurs, noon-midnight;
　　　　Fri-Sat, 12:30pm-1:30am;
　　　　Sun, 6pm-midnight

Junior Does Wine
Address: Meandrou 5, Ilisia
Telephone: +30 21 0722 2883
Hours: Tues-Sun, 6pm-1am

Materia Prima (in Koukaki)
Address: Falirou 68, Koukaki
Telephone: +30 21 0924 5935
Hours: 6pm-1:30am

Materia Prima (in Pagrati)
Address: Pl. Mesologgiou 3, Pagrati
Telephone: +30 21 0725 5171
Hours: Tues-Sun. 6pm-1:30am

Oinoscent
Address: Voulis 45-47, Syntagma
Telephone: +30 210 322 9374
Hours: Mon-Wed, 5:30pm-1am;
　　　　Thurs-Sun, 2pm-1am

CHOP SHOPS

Grilled Lamb Downtown

Greeks eat beef or pork at least once per week; lamb, however, is not an everyday thing but a treat, something more than just meat – and lamb chops, called *paidakia*, are a delicacy. Paidakia are traditionally marinated with oregano, lemon juice, thyme and pepper and then grilled at a high temperature, usually over charcoal, until they are well done. They usually come with *patates tiganites* (Greek French fries), a combo that's as irresistible as it is cholesterol-raising.

There are certain areas near Athens – Kalyvia, Varibobi, Stamata – that specialize in lamb chops, but going to them is an excursion. Luckily, central Athens has a few good places for paidakia.

In Pagrati, near the statue of President Truman, speedy and organized **Karavitis** serves typical and well executed Greek taverna fare: *saganaki* (fried cheese), wild boiled greens and Greek salad. Served piping hot, the paidakia, which come by the kilo (but you can start with a half), are remarkably succulent and have an extra-assertive charcoal flavor. Locals also swear by the *biftekia*, grilled ground beef patties filled with cheese. Karavitis's bread is a mix of sourdough and classic white bread, and the house wine is very decent for the price.

Our absolute favorite paidakia place, **To Steki tou Ilia**, is located downtown, right next to one of Athens's best art galleries (Bernier Eliades). Harried waiters bring platters full of thinly cut lamb chops to the tables lined up outside on the cobblestone street. Extremely thin but full of fat, these tantalizingly sloppy, juicy chops are robust in flavor and smoke. The eatery also serves *sykotaria*, fried lamb liver, a rare delicacy in Athens.

A final tip: Greeks eat paidakia with their hands. You can always try using a knife and fork, but it will be a waste of both your time and of good meat. Plus, there is something delightfully

primeval about sticking your teeth into a well-done, charcoal-flavored lamb chop. Perhaps that's part of what makes eating one such a treat.

Karavitis (Καραβίτης)
Address: Pafsaniou 4 (at Arktinou), Pagrati
Telephone: +30 210 721 5155
Hours: Mon-Thurs, 7pm-1:30am;
Fri-Sun, 1:30pm-1:30am

To Steki tou Ilia (first branch, Το Στέκι
Του Ηλία)
Address: Eptachalkou 5, Thiseio
Telephone: +30 210 345 8052
Hours: Mon-Sat, 1pm-1am;
Sun, 12:45-7pm

To Steki tou Ilia (second branch, Το Στέκι
Του Ηλία)
Address: Thessalonikis 7, Thiseio
Telephone: +30 210 342 2407
Hours: Mon-Sat, 6:30pm-midnight;
Sun, noon-midnight

CUP BY CUP

Central Athens's Best Coffee

What we call traditional Greek coffee is similar to the Turkish or the Middle Eastern versions, but with one big difference. It's prepared using a "blond roast" technique that roasts the coffee bean on the outside while keeping it raw on the inside, resulting in a light-colored coffee with a mild earthy flavor that's not bitter at all.

The best unfiltered Greek coffee is traditionally prepared over warm sand *(hovoli),* a method still employed at some coffee shops *(kafeneia)* around the country. In central Athens, one of these places is **Cherchez la Femme**, a beautiful kafeneio right across from the Metropolitan Cathedral. It's named after a famous old Greek song written by one of the best-known Rebetiko musicians, Vassilis Tsitsanis. For fans of floral aromas and flavors, we recommend the Greek coffee made with rosewater.

The best espresso bar in the city is with no doubt **Kaya**, a tiny coffee workshop located in Stoa Bolani (Bolani Arcade), which hides some of the best secrets of central Athens. The queue can be scary-long at times but service is fast and everyone is always in a good mood and ready to chat, making waiting to be served unexpectedly pleasant.

The Coffee Tree in Exarchia is a cozy coffee shop where you can sit and enjoy an excellent cup or glass of coffee. Here, you can buy one of the many freshly roasted, freshly ground coffee varieties from around the world that they have on sale, along with tasty cookies (one comes free with every coffee), truffles, handmade chocolates and cakes. There's a friendly vibe, a devoted customer base, and a quieter sitting area upstairs for those who wish to study, or just enjoy their coffee in peace.

Located on a picturesque pedestrian street, the beautifully designed **Underdog** in Thiseio is one of the best places to have a proper coffee in Athens, preferably in its sunny backyard. The staff's deep knowledge about coffee has been recognized

with awards in both national and international competitions, so let the talented baristas guide your selection according to your taste. Their cold brew is perfectly prepared and their "espresso tonic" is definitely an experience. Apart from their excellent coffee (which you can also buy to make at home) and stellar presentation, Underdog also offers all-day snacks, brunch, an impressive list of artisanal beers and cocktails, and coffee workshops.

Finally, we can't talk about Greek coffee without expounding on the summer classics: *frappé* and *freddo* (shaken instant coffee and double espresso over ice, respectively). While many Greeks consume both all year long, the freddo is decidedly tastier (and stronger and more sophisticated). So popular are these iced drinks that the more recent global trend of cold brew coffee has barely made a dent in Greece. While we'd only be tempted

by frappé when in a caffeine pinch, one of the best spots for freddo in central Athens is **Dope Roasting**. A trendy micro-roaster that opened in 2019, co-owner Antonis Tzaroukian oversees the coffee roasting, which is done entirely on the premises. He is a huge fan of the freddo himself, which they call cryo (**κρύο**) at Dope. Another spot for a well-crafted freddo is **Joshua Tree**, in Mets.

Cherchez La Femme (Σερσέ λα Φαμ)
Address: Mitropoleos 46, Syntagma
Telephone: +30 210 322 2029
Hours: 10am-midnight

Dope Roasting
Address: Vissis 25
Telephone: +30 210 3215209
Hours: Mon-Fri, 8am-5pm; Sat, 9am-5pm;
        Sun, 10am-5pm

Joshua Tree
Address: Anapafseos 13, Mets
Telephone: +30 210 9239747
Hours: 8am-midnight

Kaya
Address: Voulis 7 (Stoa Bolani), Syntagma
Telephone: +30 213 028 4305
Hours: Mon-Fri, 7am-4pm; Sat, 8am-3pm

The Coffee Tree (Δέντρο του Καφέ)
Address: Harilaou Trikoupi 89, Exarchia
Telephone: +30 215 550 3754
Hours: 8am-8pm, closed Sundays

Underdog
Address: Iraklidon 8, Thiseio
Telephone: +30 213 036 5393
Hours: 8am-7pm

DAILY DOUGH

Athens's Best Small Bakeries

Bread is staple in Greece, consumed on a daily basis alongside meals, or even simply with cheese. Small or family-run bakeries are always beloved in Athens, evident in the lines of people that form each morning at any neighborhood bakery. Apart from bread, bakeries also serve up an array of doughy goodies, including pies, cookies, rusks, crostinis, sandwiches and pastries.

The family-owned **Pnyka** bakery is famous for its traditional-style sourdough bread and for its hearty whole-grain loaves, made from flour the bakery mills itself at its headquarters in Pagrati. To get your hands on it, you have to get to one of its three branches in central Athens (or Vienna, if you happen to be there) early, as it sells out quickly. Pnyka sets itself apart from the chains that have taken over Athens in the last few years through its techniques and commitment to quality ingredients. Apart from the bread here, taste their famous *koulourakia* – the traditional and vegan olive oil cookies, as well

as delicious pies (savory and sweet). From the latter are the luscious and syrupy *portokalopita* (orange pie) and the *galaktoboureko* (syrupy milk custard pie).

Located in residential Koukaki, **Takis** bakery is famous for its breads, the round *koulouri* bagel typically covered in sesame seeds, cheese pies, great sandwiches and aromatic *tsoureki* (Easter bread). Customers start lining up the night before Lent to get their hands on Takis's *lagana,* a focaccia-like bread sprinkled with sesame seeds that's eaten to mark the beginning of the holiday. The bakery's flavorful *vasilopita,* a cake eaten during New Year's, is a reason to visit at the end of the year – but Takis is great any day of the week, any time of year.

The most famous place downtown for the emblematic ring-shaped koulouri is undoubtedly **To Koulouri tou Psyri**. This bakery, which is virtually open 24/7, supplies most of the koulouri stands in town and it makes a great stop for an on-the-go

breakfast – or even after a night out drinking, or to take the edge off the morning after.

If you are looking for a special kind of bakery to try something new, then think no more! **Peinirli Ionias**, in Ambelokipoi specialize in *peinirli,* yeasty boat-shaped bread with toppings (usually of the buttery or cheesy variety) baked in a wood-fired oven. We love the ground meat and cheese, in particular. Apart from the pizza-style peinirli options, which are several, you can also create your own combo. Additionally, there is a daily variety of wonderful breads, including a cheese bread, olive bread and amazing wood-oven-baked pita.

Tromero Paidi's name is inspired by the French expression "Enfant Terrible" (terrible child), which is used to describe embarrassingly candid, unconventional kids – who may prove to be wildly successful later in life, if unorthodox. A fitting moniker for a bakery with French flair that opened amidst the 2020 Covid lockdowns. The two owners and bakers, Christos and Stefanos, quit their day jobs to dedicate themselves to our daily bread. Their boutique artisanal bakery in central Athens's Ilisia sells eight

Kora
Address: Panagiotou Anagnostopoulou 44,
Kolonaki
Telephone: +30 21 0362 7855
Hours: Mon-Fri, 8am-6pm;
       Sat-Sun, 8:30am-3pm

Peinirli Ionias (Πεϊνιρλί Ιωνίας)
Address: Panormou 3, Ambelokipoi
Telephone: +30 210 6462854
Hours: Mon-Fri, 8:30am-5pm;
       Sat, 9am-3:30pm

Pnyka (Πνύκα)
Address: Pratinou 13, Pagrati
Telephone: +30 210 725 1941
Hours: Mon-Sat, 6am-9pm; Sun, 6am-4pm

Takis (Αρτοποιότης Ο Τάκης)
Address: Misaraliotou 14, Koukaki
Telephone: +30 210 923 0052
Hours: Mon-Fri, 7am-9pm; Sat, 7am-5pm

Tromero Paidi (Τρομερό Παιδί)
Address: Papadiamantopoulou 30, Ilisia
Telephone: +30 21 0777 7537
Hours: Mon-Fri, 7am-7pm; Sat, 8am-5pm

To Koulouri tou Psyri (Το Κουλούρι του
Ψυρρή)
Address: Agias Theklas 23, Psyri
Telephone: +30 210 321 5962
Hours: Open 24 hrs

different types of bread each day, and sources quality ingredients. There are multigrain baguettes, fragrant rye breads and whole wheat ones too, as well as pastries, tarts, croissants and cakes – all made in house, from scratch and with extra care.

Kora is another newcomer, this time in fancy Kolonaki. It immediately became a hit thanks to its delicious sourdough breads and excellent croissants. Their sandwiches are like no other, and unusual treats like rye cinnamon rolls are sure to pique interest, as well as classics like lemon meringue tart.

FETA ACCOMPLI

All About Greece's Big Cheese

It must be one of the world's oldest cheeses, it's certainly one of the most famous, and it's practically never missing from a Greek table, no matter the time of day. The only other food that a Greek may be even more addicted to than feta is bread.

A pillar of Greek culture and cuisine that's older than the Parthenon, feta accounts for 40 percent of cheese sales in this cheese-mad country. One reason for its popularity is its adaptability; the other, its taste – usually salty and slightly sour, neither bland nor too pungent. A curd cheese made with ewe's milk, feta is traditionally mixed with up to 30 percent goat's milk, never cow's. At cheese counters, you can ask for soft *(malaki)* or hard *(skliri)* feta; the former is creamy and milder, the latter (a bit older) is sharper and drier.

To make feta, the milk is first thickened with rennet at temperatures ranging between 24 and 36 degrees Celsius, then poured into molds to drain the whey out (fresh cheeses like *anthotyro* and *myzithra* are made with the whey). Next, it's salted and left to rest in a cold room before being put into wooden barrels filled with brine. Aging cheese in brine was a good technique in warm climates, as the salty solution prevents the formation of undesirable bacteria. Nowadays the barrels are kept in refrigerators, and by law feta must not be sold until it has been steeping for 60 days.

To start your feta education, head to **Kostarelos**, a family-run cheese deli in the Athens district of Kolonaki that has been making cheese since 1937. They source their ewe's and goat's milk from free-ranging flocks in southern Evia and still use a secret original "prescription" for homemade rennet. Their spread-like soft feta is ideal for sandwiches while the feta aged for 12 months is an artisanal table cheese with multilayered flavor that could easily hold its own alongside brie and gorgonzola. With a large selection of other cheeses and other nibbles from small producers

around the country, Kostarelos is an appealing place to grab a bite and a glass of wine. The menu even has a glossary to aid visitors in ordering.

I **Feta tis Hiras**, which in Greek means "The Widow's Feta," is a tiny little store near Piraeus port that has been running since 1936. That year, Mrs. Sotiria's husband – who operated a small cheese-making studio from their home – passed away. She then opened her own cheese shop, at a time when owning a business was not easy for a woman, muchless one newly single. I Feta tis Hiras is now run by Mrs. Sotiria's grandson Thomas and his partners. His grandmother's homemade feta, anthotyros, graviera and yogurt have been carefully replaced with cheeses sourced from

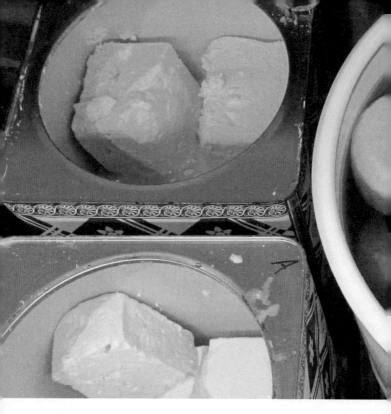

small producers. Particularly famous is their creamy, buttery feta from Argos, and the anthotyros and mizithra from Amfilochia. Other artisanal and small production products from around the country are also available here, such as top-quality cold cuts, fresh butter and honey.

Love cheese but want a taste beyond feta? Our favorite deli in the central market area is the hole-in-the-wall Arapian, along with its sibling, **Ta Karamanlidika tou Fani**, on the corner opposite (the businesses now share the same name after the passing of Mr. Arapian).

Although they now offer a wide selection of meats and cheeses, sourced from artisanal producers all over the country, the shop mainly sold

air-dried cured meats like *pastourma* and *soutzouki,* before branching out. Now you can find aged gravieras smoked or studded with peppercorns, and medium-soft kasseri goat cheeses flavored with different herbs and spices. Take your time choosing what you want, don't be afraid to ask about any of the products on display, and by all means taste before you buy.

I Feta tis Hiras (Η φέτα της χήρας)
Address: Aristidou 25, Piraeus
Telephone: +30 210 417 0449

Kostarelos (Κωσταρέλος)
Address: Patriarchou Ioakeim 30-32,
        Kolonaki
Telephone: +30 210 725 9000
Web: www.kostarelos.gr
Hours: Mon-Fri, 8am-9pm;
       Sat, 8am-8pm; Sun, 10am-8pm

Ta Karamanlidika tou Fani (Τα Καραμανλίδικα του Φάνη)
Address: Sokratous 1 & Evripidou 52
Telephone: +30 210 325 4184
Hours: 8am-11pm, closed Sundays

GELATO GOES GREEK

The Best Gelato Spots in Athens

In a country where half the year we live like it's summer, ice cream and gelato are about as popular as they can get. Gelato can be easily found around the city and even late into the night, but these days, much of what is called "artisanal gelato" is generally prepared using ready-made industrial powder mixes that contain artificial colorings, flavors, margarine, preservatives and other additives to enhance flavor, improve structure and prolong shelf life.

However, our favorite downtown Athens spots source the finest ingredients and fresh fruit to prepare seasonal flavors and wonderful sorbets, as well as creative and unusual combinations that any gelato-lover is bound to adore.

Opened in July 2014 near Syntagma Square, **Le Greche** can be blamed for starting the trend of high-quality gelato in Athens. Owner Evi Papadopoulou is still committed to using quality, fresh, all-natural products, impeccably sourced from Greece and Italy. Only the best ingredients make it through the doors of her laboratory, and then they are put through a series of blind taste tests to determine the best flavor combinations and uses. She makes her gelato from scratch according to classic Italian recipes. The rest of their process is top secret and uniquely Le Greche's own. The proof is in this frozen pudding: velvety-textured, well-balanced and flavorful. Here is top gelato. Among our favorite flavors are the pistachio, the fiore di latte, the figs with mascarpone (made with the finest figs from Kalamata), and the fresh lemon and mint sorbet. La Greche also has two other branches, one in Agia Paraskevi and another in Psychiko.

In Koukaki, near the Acropolis Metro Station, **Django** is a must visit gelato spot, where – even in bad weather – you will probably find a long line of people waiting to be served. We are particularly endeared to Django because, beyond its excellent, 100%

natural gelato and sorbets, they also offer half scoops – meaning more room to try more flavors! You can see them preparing the gelato in their open kitchen/workshop. Their first shop opened on Syros Island in 2005 and, following their huge success there, they opened a branch in Athens in 2021. Sustainably minded, their motto is "ethics above profit." Their gelato is made daily in-house, and you may happen to find unique seasonal flavors such as quince, fig or watermelon sorbets. From their "pantry" shop, you can source some of the fine ingredients they use in their gelatos, like the chocolate and vanilla beans, as well as traditional treats from Syros.

Kokkion is a miniscule ice-cream shop in Psyri, near Monastiraki. They source their milk from northern Greece and their fine chocolate from France. We love their take on the traditional Greek *kaimaki* flavor (sheep's milk and mastic), which they prepare with aromatic mastic from Chios and rich Buffalo milk

sourced from the Kerkini lake region in northern Greece. The yogurt flavor is also great, prepared with sheep's milk yogurt from Lesvos. Here, you will also find plenty of gluten-free and vegan options, such as the popular almond and tonka bean flavor, or their tangerine with ginger sorbet. They also have a selection of ice lollies and in-house prepared desserts sold in jars, such as almond tiramisu and profiteroles.

Epik Gelato is located in Mavili Square near the American Embassy. Here, they specialize in flavors inspired from traditional Greek treats and products. The ingredients are carefully sourced from artisanal producers – take, for instance, the milk and yogurt from a nunnery near Corinth. Their pistachio flavor, made with the famous Aegina island pistachios, is a best-seller here. It comes in two hard-to-choose

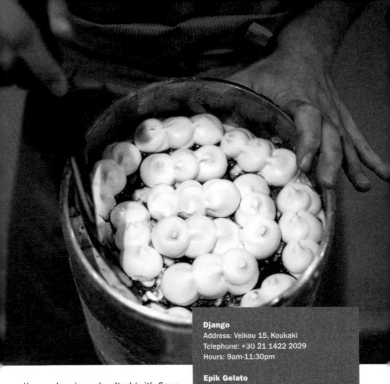

options; classic and salted (with fleur de sel from Mani in the southern Peloponnese). Other flavors worth trying are the rose *loukoumi* (Turkish delight) as well as the Ikaria figs and *katiki* cheese (a fresh creamy cheese from Domokos). Old-school desserts are made funky as well, such as *Armenoville,* a classic treat from Thessaloniki, made with semifreddo cream, chopped caramelized almonds, and crumbled meringue.

Django
Address: Veikou 15, Koukaki
Telephone: +30 21 1422 2029
Hours: 9am-11:30pm

Epik Gelato
Address: Dorileou 2, Mavili Square
Telephone: +30 21 0646 4105
Hours: 11am-midnight

Kokkion
Address: Protogenous 2, Psyri
Telephone: +30 6981563511
Hours: Mon-Fri, 8am-midnight;
      Sat-Sun, 10am-midnight

Le Greche
Address: Mitropoleos 16, Syntagma
Telephone: +30 216 700 6458
Hours: Mon-Thurs, 8:30am-midnight;
      Fri-Sun, 8:30am-1am

THE GIVING TREE

An Intro to Greek Olive Oil

In Greece, where the land is mostly rocky and steep and the climate hot and arid, the olive tree thrives, and for millennia, olive oil has been as essential to Greek cooking as the gnarled, silver-leaved trees have been to its landscape. Greece is the third largest producer of olive oil in the world after Spain and Italy and the greatest in consumption per capita. Around 75% of Greek olive oil production is extra virgin which means that the term "extra virgin" is a norm for Greeks.

Koroneiki, the most famous Greek olive variety, is mostly grown in the Peloponnese and Crete, and the oil made from it tends to be pungent, fruity, spicy and slightly bitter – ideal for all uses. Athinolia is grown in the same areas as Koroneiki, but its more intense fruitiness and balanced peppery and bitter notes makes it suited to drizzling on food just before serving. Grown mainly in the Peloponnese, the Manaki variety is mild and used in everyday cooking and frying, while Valanolia, cultivated on the islands of Lesbos and Chios, offers complex aromas and a strong fruity flavor and is also suitable for cooking.

Whatever oil you take home, be sure to store it in a dark and cool place, ideally in a tightly shut glass or tin vessel to keep the contents from oxidizing and going rancid. The fresher the better: It's best to consume the olive oil within six to 12 months.

In Athens, one of our favorite places for olive oil is **Malotira**, near the Metropolitan Cathedral of Athens. It specializes exclusively in carefully selected high quality extra virgin olive oils and the well-trained staff will always be ready to fill you up with as much information as you can hold. As those who have joined our Plaka food walk know, you can experience a professional olive oil tasting here as the owners of the shop are certified olive oil sommeliers. They carefully select excellent quality extra virgin

and high phenolic olive oils made by small producers around Greece. Their selection includes internationally awarded brands such as The Governor from Corfu and Pamako from Crete. Apart from the olive oils here, you will find a selection of premium honeys and other fine products from Greece.

In Kolonaki, a few minutes walk from the Greek Parliament, **Yolenis** is a large deli with a wide selection of Greek delicacies including olive oils and olives. They feature products from all around Greece made by small and larger producers, while their selection of olive oil is quite diverse, with oils of all varieties and regions. Apart from the regular extra virgin and high phenolic olive oils on sale here, they also have wild olive tree olive oil from Sparta, and early harvest olive oils, as well as a lovely

selection of aromatic olive oils, like truffle, oregano or basil. They also have a navigable e-shop which ships to Europe and the US.

Pantopoleio Moiropoulos Dimitrios George is a lovely little deli in Exarchia, and it is definitely one of our favorite spots in Athens to shop for goodies, particularly from the region of Mani and Messenia in the southern Peloponnese – both big olive oil regions. Dimitris, the owner who inherited this wonderful business from his father, is proud of his fine products, particularly the olives. They come from Messenia and are of the Koroneiki variety: aromatic, fruity and pleasantly spicy. Here, you will also get the best Kalamata olives you can find in a store, and beautiful *siglino* (cured pork) and sausage with orange from Mani.

Mandragoras, in the Piraeus port, is one of the most historic delis in town. Among a vast selection of local artisanal and traditional products, you'll find carefully selected olive oil brands, mainly from the Peloponnese region in southern Greece, that are sure to impress. If you go for the olive oils, make sure to taste their olives and have a look at the dried Greek herbs, which are also excellent.

Malotira (Μαλοτήρα)
Address: Apollonos 30, Plaka
Telephone: + 30 210 3246008
Hours: Mon-Sat, 11am-6:30pm

Mandragoras (Μανδραγόρας)
Address: Dim. Gounari 14-16, Piraeus
Telephone: +30 210 417 2961
Hours: Sat-Wed, 8am-4:30pm;
Thurs-Fri, 8:30pm

**Pantopoleio Moiropoulos Dimitrios
George** (Μοιρόπουλος Δημήτρης)
Address: Gravias 2, Exarchia
Telephone: +30 21 0381 8846
Hours: Mon-Fri, 9am-6pm; Sat, 9am-4pm

Yolenis Greek Gastronomy Center
Address: Solonos 9, Kolonaki
Telephone: +30 21 2222 3623
Hours: 8am-midnight

GREEK WILD HERBS

A Shopper's Guide

Due to its temperate climate and exceptionally diverse flora and fauna, Greece is one of the richest countries in the world, herbally speaking. Wild herbs, usually collected from mountains, are used for teas and infusions – the majority of them intended as natural remedies – and for cooking and baking.

Here, we've listed a few of the most-popular Greek herbs and described their uses. Of course, they can neither replace medicine nor are they meant to be consumed in extreme quantities. You may also wish to check first for allergic reactions.

Recently claimed to be a natural weapon against Alzheimer's disease, *tsai tou vunu*, or mountain tea, can also aid the upper respiratory system, fend off colds and has other notable antimicrobial and antioxidant properties. Look for the dried leaves of plants of the genus *Sideritis*, which grow on the slopes of Mt. Olympus.

Chamomile *(chamomili)* can be applied as a poultice to calm skin irritations. Brewed as a tea, it can help settle an upset stomach or aid in sleep. Another herb used for relaxation is louisa, or lemon verbena. For stimulation, there's *faskomilo* (sage) tea, and for headaches and migraines, drink a cup of strong *fliskouni* (wild mint) tea.

Dictamo (Origanum dictamnus, or dittany) is a wild plant native to Crete. It has a very strong, pleasant fragrance and flavor and soothes an upset digestive system as well as headaches and toothaches. It's a relative of oregano, which is perhaps the most commonly used herb in the Greek kitchen and rich in vitamin C.

Evripidou Street, near the central market, is Athens's herb and spice district. In many stores, small bunches of dried herbs hang on the walls, giving off the scent of the Greek countryside. At **Elixir**, beautiful antique wooden cases hold the rarest of herbs. Owner Periklis Koniaris and his wife offer expert guidance to the

uninitiated or curious.

Batavia, a sophisticated grocery store specializing in herbs and teas, has four shops strategically placed throughout Athens and the suburbs, but the best one is in the bustling neighborhood of Kallithea.

Our preferred guide to Greek wild herbs, however, is Stefanos Papatziallas, owner of **Madras** teahouse in Piraeus (as well as a new location in Syntagma). He sources all his tea directly from producers in Asia and Africa, as well as from all over Greece. At Madras, you can compare mountain teas from the island of Euboea to those from the Magnesia area in Thessaly. For

Batavia
Address: Gripari 138, Kallithea
Telephone: +30 210 953 1042
Hours: Mon-Fri, 8am-8:30pm;
Sat, 8am-5pm

Elixir (Ελιξήριον)
Address: Evripidou 41, Downtown
Telephone: +30 210 321 5141
Hours: 8am-3pm, closed Sundays

Madras (Piraeus)
Address: Notara 21, Piraeus
Telephone: +30 210 411 80 67
Hours: Mon & Wed, 8am-4pm;
Tues, Thurs & Fri, 8am-8pm;
Sat, 8am-3pm

Madras (Syntagma)
Address: Voulis 7, Syntagma
Telephone: +30 210 324 27 77
Hours: Mon & Wed, 10am-4pm;
Tues, Thurs & Fri, 10am-7pm;
Sat, 10am-3pm

Mandragoras (Μανδραγόρας)
Address: Dim. Gounari 14-16, Piraeus
Telephone: +30 210 417 2961
Hours: Sat-Wed, 8am-4:30pm;
Thurs-Fri, 8:30pm

anyone wishing to dive deep into the world of tea, Papatziallas will happily share everything he knows. Also in Piraeus is **Mandragoras**. We already proselytized their olive oils, but their selection of dried Greek herbs are excellent – as they should be, considering how long they have been around.

GREEK YOGURT

The Real Deal

"Greek yogurt" has in recent years become a global phenomenon. In Greece, it's simply known as yogurt and it puts whatever you've had elsewhere to shame.

First, a few basics: Traditional Greek yogurt is usually made from sheep's milk. Its high fat content gives it a thick, creamy consistency and distinct richness and flavor that vary according to how the animal it came from was raised. It has a slightly sour taste and leaves a fresh sensation in the mouth. "Live" yogurt consists of just two ingredients, milk and bacteria culture, and consequently has a shorter shelf life than the industrial version.

In Greece, yogurt is usually served cold. It can be eaten on its own or as part of any meal: with honey, walnuts and a dash of cinnamon for breakfast, with chunks of fresh fruit as a light meal, or as the foundation of salad dressings or sauces such as tzatziki. Yogurt often accompanies a bowl of white rice, a plate of French fries or a piece of savory pie. As a light dessert, it's topped with spoon sweets (traditional fruit preserves).

Usually sold in clay or plastic pots, yogurt can be found everywhere from supermarkets to dairy bars. When we're in the mood to sit down and enjoy our yogurt in a wonderfully atmospheric setting, we head to the dairy bar **Stani**, which has been in business in Omonia since 1931, or to the equally retro **Stani Kountoura**, in Piraeus. We also love **Bakoyiannis**, in Ilioupoli, opened by Vasilis Bakoyiannis back in 1954. His son, Yannis, who has taken over the business, recalls him tooling around Athens on a tricycle, distributing fresh milk and yogurt that came from animals that grazed on the pastures of what is now Nea Peramos, in West Attica. All the Bakoyiannis products – including cream and rice pudding – are magnificent, but the yogurt with its thick, voluptuous top layer and distinctive, tangy flavor reigns supreme.

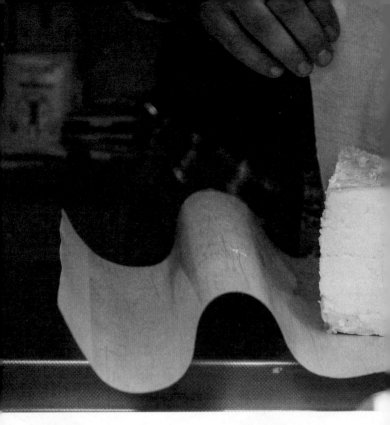

Also in Ilioupoli, the butcher shop **Ravanis** is popular not just for meat but also for its exceptional and hard-to-find ice cream, made of sheep's milk, and, of course, its traditionally produced yogurt. Open since 1915, **Afoi Asimakopouloi** in Exarchia, a third-generation family-owned pastry shop, is famous for its homemade

dairy products, especially its yogurt, butter and rice pudding. (The extraordinary quality of that butter is evident in the Greek-style baklava sold here, a whole other story.)

Theodosios Mavroyiannis started **Karyas Dairy** in the picturesque village of Karya, 30 km from Argos. His family also runs a cheerful, pint-

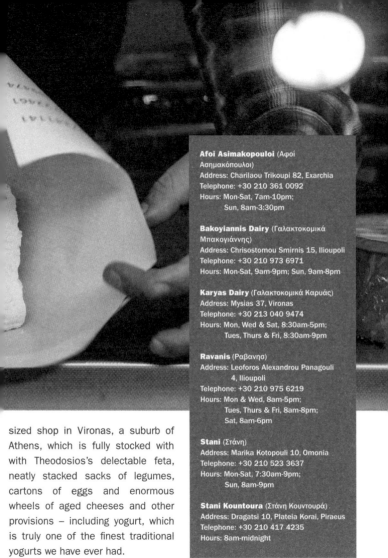

Afoi Asimakopouloi (Αφοί Ασημακόπουλοι)
Address: Charilaou Trikoupi 82, Exarchia
Telephone: +30 210 361 0092
Hours: Mon-Sat, 7am-10pm;
Sun, 8am-3:30pm

Bakoyiannis Dairy (Γαλακτοκομικά Μπακογιάννης)
Address: Chrisostomou Smirnis 15, Ilioupoli
Telephone: +30 210 973 6971
Hours: Mon-Sat, 9am-9pm; Sun, 9am-8pm

Karyas Dairy (Γαλακτοκομικά Καρυάς)
Address: Mysias 37, Vironas
Telephone: +30 213 040 9474
Hours: Mon, Wed & Sat, 8:30am-5pm;
Tues, Thurs & Fri, 8:30am-9pm

Ravanis (Ραβανησ)
Address: Leoforos Alexandrou Panagouli 4, Ilioupoli
Telephone: +30 210 975 6219
Hours: Mon & Wed, 8am-5pm;
Tues, Thurs & Fri, 8am-8pm;
Sat, 8am-6pm

Stani (Στάνη)
Address: Marika Kotopouli 10, Omonia
Telephone: +30 210 523 3637
Hours: Mon-Sat, 7:30am-9pm;
Sun, 8am-9pm

Stani Kountoura (Στάνη Κουντουρά)
Address: Dragatsi 10, Plateia Korai, Piraeus
Telephone: +30 210 417 4235
Hours: 8am-midnight

sized shop in Vironas, a suburb of Athens, which is fully stocked with with Theodosios's delectable feta, neatly stacked sacks of legumes, cartons of eggs and enormous wheels of aged cheeses and other provisions – including yogurt, which is truly one of the finest traditional yogurts we have ever had.

GREEN SCENE

Athenian Gardens of Eating (and Drinking)

Modern urban development has not been particularly gentle with Athens, but thankfully, there are some oases in the cement desert that offer the hungry local or tourist a lush respite in which to enjoy a meal or a drink.

A few steps away from the Syntagma metro, a heavy iron gate stands guard over the former residence of the German archaeologist Heinrich Schliemann, now home to the **Numismatic Museum**. Its beautiful garden still includes many species of Greek flora. Fortify yourself for a walk with some seafood mezes: We recommend the *avgotaraho,* a cured and dried mullet roe with a chewy, velvety texture that smelled intensely, and pleasantly, of the sea. Boldly flavored sardine fillets on toast with slightly peppery Cretan cheese were a wonderful accompaniment to a glass of white wine.

The **Black Duck Garden**, located on Klauthmonos Square, is housed in one of the city's oldest surviving neoclassical buildings, the temporary palace of King Otto and Queen Amalia, who planted its once-massive garden herself. Today, the garden is much smaller, and Black Duck shares the building with the City of Athens Museum. Food is served between 10 a.m. and 7 p.m. There's breakfast, brunch, all-day snacks like sandwiches, cheese platters, and fresh salads and main dishes with royal flair – like the slow-roasted guinea fowl served with carrot purée, black sesame seeds and pickled carrots.

Less than a five-minute walk from the Monastiraki metro, **Six D.O.G.S.** ("Degrees of Global Separation") is a cultural venue that includes an urban garden, performance space, bar and project space that hosts everything from art exhibitions to clothing swaps. A neon sign directed us down the stairs to a place that genuinely felt like a secret hideout. We enjoyed the refreshing, just-sweet-enough lemonade and sour cherry juice, both

made in-house, and shared a fresh and fluffy tiramisu. We'll go back for their popular bagels, three kinds of pizza, nachos with homemade guacamole and the hot D.O.G.S. Everything is prepared fresh daily from seasonal ingredients.

For those feeling more adventurous, a 6.5-km ride outside Athens's bustling city center lies a beautiful, lush forest with ancient paths and Byzantine monuments – and **Kalopoula Refreshments**, a little canteen where you can enjoy lunch near an ancient spring. In a forest on Ymittos Mountain, a 30-minute walk from the Kaisariani Cemetery and off the Kaisariani Monastery

loop trail is this bustling picnic area and well-kept Athens secret. The Kalopoula spring gurgles and froths, as picnickers and hikers take a break to some surprisingly delicious, traditional Greek food like *saganaki* (fried cheese), *kayianas* (eggs with tomatoes), fried meatballs, Greek salad and pies from a local bakery.

Numismatic Museum Café
Address: El. Venizelou (Panepistimiou) 12, Syntagma
Telephone: + 30 210 361 0067
Hours: 9am-11pm

The Black Duck Garden
Address: I. Paparigopoulou 5-7, Kauthmonos Square
Telephone: +30 210 325 2396
Hours: Thurs-Tues, 10am-6:30pm; Wed, 10am-11:30pm

Six D.O.G.S.
Address: Avramiotou 6-8, Monastiraki
Telephone: +30 210 321 0510
Hours: Sun-Thurs, 11am-2:30am; Fri, 11am-4:30am

Kalopoula Refreshments (Αναψυκτήριο Καλοπούλα)
Address: Zografou 161 22, Kaisariani Forest (Buses 223 and 224 finish at Kaisariani Cemetery, and then it's about 30 min walking, or a short taxi ride)
Hours: 7:30am-5pm

GRILL TALK

Downtown Souvlaki Joints

While Athens's more upscale neighborhoods have recently rediscovered the gastronomic joys – and, let's face it, the economic sense – of eating souvlaki, this dish has never gone out of fashion in downtown Athens.

Kostas, an unassuming souvlaki joint on Pentelis Street, two blocks from Syntagma Square, is our personal favorite. The meat is of exceptional quality and is juicy without being greasy; this means that, unlike at most other souvlaki joints, here you can eat more than one. The pita bread, which is fat-free, is stuffed with either souvlaki or a kebab and then topped with thinly sliced pieces of onion, full-fat strained yogurt, tomato and plenty of parsley. The result is as light and fresh as it gets.

Hidden away in Satovriandou, a neighborhood filled with boarded-up storefronts located right behind Omonia Square, **Lefteris o Politis** has been in business since 1951 and has remained unchanged since it opened.

There is only one kind of souvlaki on offer here, and it is spectacular. It's a spicy meat kebab made solely of beef, unlike most kebabs, which are usually a combination of veal, lamb and sometimes pork, and cooked on a traditional grill. It's a dish for purists: beef kebab, tomato, thinly sliced onion and parsley wrapped in grilled pita. Despite the lack of sauce, the whole package is satisfyingly spicy and succulent.

Giorgos-Manos is much less well known and a totally different animal. It's located in Exarchia, Athens's most turbulent yet interesting neighborhood, and a hub for intellectuals and students alike. This is the rare souvlaki joint that keeps banking hours. Giorgos-Manos has the typical setup, with wood paneling, some pictures from old Greek movies on top of the grill, a few seats and an extremely loyal clientele. Although Athenians like to eat their lunch late, this place is packed from 11 a.m. onwards.

The souvlaki offerings are plentiful. The pork and chicken gyro and *kalamaki* (skewered pieces of meat) are very popular, but Giorgos-Manos's specialty is the hard-to-find *kontosouvli,* large chunks of pork usually from the upper shoulder that are marinated for at least 12 hours in anything from onion juice to oregano, garlic or paprika and then placed on skewers. They offer a chicken kontosouvli as well, but we prefer the old-fashioned original, and we recommend getting it wrapped in pita with tzatziki, onion and parsley.

To find **Elvis** in the lively neighborhood of Metaxourgeio you can either follow the music or the

enticing smells of the grill to lead you there. The owners keep the menu brief and to the point, with only five plate options: pork or chicken souvlaki, ground beef or lamb kebab, and country-style sausage and pancetta – all grilled to perfection over charcoal and served on charming metal plates, topped with grilled pita and lots of hand-cut, freshly cooked French fries (accompanied by Elvis's famous lemon-mustard sauce).

An old-school souvlaki joint beside the busy Varvakios Market, **Volvi's** minimalist menu offers classic grilled pork souvlaki or *soutzoukakia,*

Elvis (Έλβις, first branch)
Address: Plateon 29 (near Leonidou),
Metaxourgeio
Telephone: +30 210 345 5836
Hours: Sun-Thurs, noon-2:30am;
Fri-Sat, noon-2am

Elvis (Έλβις, second branch)
Address: Archimidous 1-5, Plastira Square,
Pagrati
Telephone: +30 210 345 5836
Hours: Wed-Mon, 9am-5pm;
Tues, noon-5pm

Giorgos-Manos (Γιώργος - Μάνος)
Address: Themistokleous 39, Exarchia
Telephone: +30 210 381 5442
Hours: 10am-5:30pm;
closed Saturday & Sunday

Kostas (Σουβλάκι Κώστας)
Address: Pentelis 5 (intersection with
Mitropoleos), Plaka/Syntagma
Telephone: +30 210 322 8502
Hours: 10am-3:45pm; closed Sunday

Lefteris o Politis (Λευτέρης ο Πολίτης)
Address: Satovriandou 20, Omonia
Telephone: +30 210 522 5676
Hours: Mon-Fri, 11am-7pm;
Sat, 11am-5:30pm

Volvi (Η Βόλβη)
Evripidou 24, Varvakios Market
Telephone: +30 21 1118 0587
Hours: Mon-Fri, noon-10pm;
Sat, noon-6pm

cumin garlic meatballs. Both options come in freshly baked pita or on a plate. You're bound to gobble both up so quickly you won't mind it's standing room only. Warning: The food is often so good we order seconds. Washed down by a cold Greek beer, of course.

A LIFE OF PIE

Savory Pie Shops in Athens

Greek pies – we should be clear, mostly savory ones – have long played an important role in the cuisine of the region. From as far back as the 5th century BC, Athenians enjoyed snacking on pies while watching theater or attending a public speech. Now, it's common to see locals walking around the streets of Athens with a pie in hand, especially in the morning, and they make for a perfectly acceptable main course or even dessert, when sweet.

Most rustic pies reflect the ideal of the Mediterranean diet: wheat-based phyllo, seasonal veggies, fresh herbs, high-quality cheese (when included), and olive oil. Meat-based pies are also popular, commonly featuring chicken or minced meat (usually pork and beef) and, often, lamb. The pie-making tradition and recipes evolved over the years, particularly along regional lines. Almost every part of Greece is known for its own local take on pie – for example, in the north you can find phyllo brushed with butter instead of olive oil. There are some general similarities, though: Pies in Greece are usually enclosed and savory, though of course there are many exceptions.

You'll find plenty of pie shops all around the city, but our favorites serve up the more homemade, rustic versions, where the phyllo is a bit thicker, not greasy or heavy, and the ingredients are fresh and seasonal. Like those that Harris and Yiouli, who have been married for almost half a century, make at **Harry's Kitchen**. Harris is in charge of the phyllo and Yiouli makes the different fillings, fresh every day. Try their delicious cheese pie made with three Greek cheeses, mint and scallions. Their meat pie is also delicious, made with a mix of minced pork and beef. If you want to try a sweet version, go for the apple pie, made with fresh chunks of apple and served warm, sprinkled with a generous amount of cinnamon and powdered sugar.

In Exarchia, **Filomila** sells vegetarian and vegan Greek-style

pies and tarts, plus some dishes of the day. The fillings feature tasty combinations like red lentils, spinach and beets or peppers, figs and cheese – and the flavors change daily. Owner Efstathia makes dozens of savory tarts and pies each morning, plus a couple of sweet ones.

A historic place for pie in Athens, **Ariston** means "excellent" in Greek. Tucked into the extremely busy Voulis Street right behind Syntagma Square, this shop has been in the same spot since 1910, and is still owned by the family that opened it. Customers usually head over for the store's specialty – *kourou* pies – which are kept warm inside a rectangular glass incubator, like precious babes. These small pies shaped like half-moons are made with a solid, pastry-like dough with a feta filling, and have an almost

yellow glow. Kourou phyllo dough usually contains yogurt and butter, and this is unmistakably reflected in the taste. The butter-rich dough and the hearty dose of feta make for a heavy, salty pastry that crumbles in the mouth and is the equivalent of a full meal.

Located in the heart of Psyri, between Monastiraki and the central food market, is a pie shop specializing in *bougatsa,* the popular pie from the northern cities of Thessaloniki and Serres. At **Bougatsadiko I Thessaloniki stou Psyri**, bougatsa is made with butter and the phyllo is multilayered and crispy, resembling puff pastry a bit. The typical fillings here are feta, minced pork and beef, or a sweet version with a milk custard, served with cinnamon and powdered sugar.

On a beautiful pedestrian street in the heart of Kolonaki, **Cocona**'s owner Ioanna can be found rolling out pastry dough for her *gozleme* and delicious

enclosed pies. Of the latter, we love the minced beef, tomato and kasseri cheese and the *hortopita* made with fresh spinach, chopped leeks and Mediterranean hartwort and chervil. The gozleme is a special kind of pie brought by Greek refugees from Asia Minor in the early 1920s. It's a thin, almost crepe-like pastry stuffed and folded over, then grilled on a *sachi*, a convex cooktop. Ioanna's gozleme are made to order, and if you're particularly hungry, you can add a fried egg on top.

Ariston (Άριστον)
Address: Voulis 10, Syntagma
Telephone: +30 210 322 7626
Hours: Mon, Wed & Sat, 7:30am-6pm;
    Tues, Thurs & Fri, 7:30am-8pm

Cocona
Address: Milioni 10, Kolonaki
Telephone: +30 21 0364 6563
Hours: 9am-7pm, closed Sundays

Filomila (Φιλομήλα)
Address: Andrea Metaxa 13, Exarchia
Telephone: +30 211 409 9422
Hours: Mon-Fri, noon-6:30pm;
    Sat, noon-5:30pm

Harry's Kitchen
Address: Axarlian 2, Syntagma
Telephone: +30 211 115 2864
Hours: 7am-3pm

Bougatsadiko I Thessaloniki stou Psyri (Μπουγατσάδικο η Θεσσαλονίκη στου Ψυρρή)
Address: Pl. Iroon 1, Psyri
Telephone: +30 21 0322 2088
Hours: 7am-1am

MARKET TREASURES

Gems of the Central Market District

For the food-loving tourist, city markets and the shops around them can hold far more allure than monuments, museums and elite boutiques. Even as longtime residents of Athens, we're still regularly drawn to the Central Market district between Monastiraki and Omonia Squares, and have devoted entire days to its treasures. Athens's Central Food Market, known as Varvakios Market, is located only a few meters away from the Athens City Hall. Hidden inside the many corners of the building that houses the meat and fish market (inaugurated in 1974), you'll find several eateries of varying sizes serving meze with *ouzo* or *tsipouro*, soups and other daily dishes. **Epirus**, an all-day-and-night eatery known for its hangover-recovery soups, is a favorite of ours and a popular stop for locals in the early hours of the morning to conclude a boozy night out on the town. Their specialties include traditional boiled goat, or *gida vrasti* – a broth made

with feet and tripe (usually pork in Greece), fish soup, chicken soup and of course *mageiritsa* – a soup made from chopped lamb liver and intestines with greens, plenty of scallions and dill, and an egg-and-lemon sauce.

At one entrance to this market building, we recommend the mouthwatering grilled pork souvlaki at **Volvi** alongside a cold beer. For a different twist, **Feyrouz** on Karori Street specializes in souvlaki-style wrapped *lahmacun*, a thin flatbread with meat, vegetarian and even vegan topping options. Just across the street, they've also opened a corner pastry shop/cafe with great coffee and scrumptious, syrupy desserts like baklava.

On Aiolou Street, right behind the market, there is **Krinos**, one of the oldest cafes in Athens. Since 1923, they've specialized in *loukoumades*, airy fried balls of dough drizzled in a sweet syrup and sprinkled with cinnamon.

Stroll around the outside of the market building to find small shops selling the typical ingredients you'd need to prepare the local cuisine: cheese, eggs, all sorts of nuts and dried fruit, herbs, spices, coffee, sweet treats and more.

Across the street is the fruit and vegetable market, alongside shops selling all sorts of delicacies, such as dried, cured or smoked fish and meat, as well as pickles, cheeses, olives, sausages, breads, caviar and halva.

Evripidou is our favorite street in the neighborhood. Here, you'll find almost anything your heart desires (and plenty it may not), sold by herb and spice emporia heralded with garlands of flamboyantly colored dried vegetable casings to stuff and cook, bright chili peppers, sun-

dried tomatoes and okra. There are several such shops, each more enticing than the next. For those interested in checking out Cretan delicacies, head to **Zouridakis**. Here are cheeses, traditional pasta, olive oil and even snails from our favorite foodie island. On this street, you'll also find the wonderful delis Miran and **Ta Karamanlidika tou Fani**, a much larger store-cum-all-day-restaurant. Among the best delis in town, these shops specialize in cured meats and cold-cuts, as well as domestic cheeses and other traditional products made by small producers.

Walk along Athinas Street amongst shops selling hardware, potted plants and birds, and whet

Epirus
Address: Filopoimenos 4
Telephone: +30 210 324 0773
Hours: 6am-8pm, closed Sundays

Feyrouz
Address: Karori 23
Telephone: +30 21 3031 8060
Hours: noon-10pm; closed Sundays

Krinos (Κρίνος)
Address: Aiolou 87
Telephone: +30 210 321 6852
Hours: Mon, Wed & Sat, 9am-7:30pm;
        Tues, Thurs-Fri, 9am-9:30pm

Ta Karamanlidika tou Fani (Τα
Καραμανλίδικα του Φάνη)
Address: Sokratous 1 & Evripidou 52
Telephone: +30 210 325 4184
Hours: 8am-11pm, closed Sundays

Volvi (Η Βόλβη)
Evripidou 24
Telephone: +30 21 1118 0587
Hours: Mon-Fri, noon-10pm;
        Sat, noon-6pm

Zouridakis (Ζουριδακησ)
Address: Evripidou 25
Telephone: +30 210 321 1109
Hours: 7am-6pm, closed Sundays

your appetite at any of the tempting bakeries, falafel stands and souvlaki joints along the way.

Weaving in and out of the alleys branching off the market will introduce you to international specialties you may be tempted to squeeze into your already full suitcase. And be sure to have your camera at the ready for unique, colorful photo ops, too.

MUSEUM RESTAURANTS

Artful Dining

Athens was late in bringing excellent dining to its museums, but now offers a host of excellent options.

Situated on the second floor, the **Acropolis Museum restaurant** is a vast, minimalist affair in shades of gray and black. A concrete, partially shaded triangular terrace offers one of the best views of Athens: The old buildings of the Makrygianni neighborhood frame none other than the Parthenon.

The menu offers creative Greek regional cooking. Instead of being spit-roasted and sliced vertically, pork gyro meat is baked and served with a strong yogurt dip, thinly sliced onion and roasted tomato. It's mushy, messy and absolutely delicious. Equally good are the salads, such as one with spinach, arugula and *siglino,* pork that is cured and smoked before being steeped in wine and preserved with pork fat and orange peel.

The restaurant stays open until midnight on Fridays, and a special breakfast menu is served until noon every day the museum is open. The breakfast here is noteworthy because it focuses on interesting, hard-to-find traditional dishes: olives from Kalamata with small rusks from Kythera, *strapatsada,* or scrambled eggs, with sweet gruyère from Naxos.

In posh Kolonaki, the **Benaki Museum** works like a crash course in Greek history, with artifacts ranging from antiquity to modern Greece. The restaurant has a breathtaking view of the National Gardens and wooded Ardittos Hill. It's popular with the ladies-who-lunch set and other sophisticated locals.

Main courses range from typical dishes like stuffed tomatoes and peppers to the more international, such as a sea bass fillet with citrus sauce and lemon blossom. Most popular are the *dolmadakia* from the island of Kasos; these tiny stuffed grape leaves come with a refreshing yogurt dip.

Two blocks down, the Museum of Cycladic Art – an old, neoclassical

building that houses an excellent collection of Cycladic, Ancient Greek and Cypriot art – has a sleek little café, the **Cycladic Café**, in a beautiful atrium filled with greenery. Meanwhile, the **Basil & Elise Goulandris Foundation** is a stunning new modern art museum in Pagrati, featuring the private collection of Basil and Elise Goulandris housed in a 1920s neoclassical mansion. The permanent exhibitions include famous masterpieces by Picasso, Matisse, Klee, Cézanne, El Greco, Renoir, Kandinsky and more. Between the first and ground floor of the villa there is a "hidden" urban garden with a beautiful cafe. It makes for a great

all-day spot for a quiet coffee or a glass of wine (especially considering the excellent selections on the wine list).

Finally, the **National Archeological Museum**, perhaps Greece's most important museum in terms of artifacts, has two cafés, one located in an open-air courtyard inside the museum, where ancient statues peek out from among the trees. Though the food (mostly basics like sandwiches

Acropolis Museum Restaurant
Address: Dionysiou Areopagitou 15, Plaka
Telephone: +30 210 900 0915
Hours: Mon-Thurs, 9am-5pm;
      Fri-Sat, 9am-midnight;
      Sun, 9am-8pm
Web: www.theacropolismuseum.gr

**Basil & Elise Goulandris Foundation
Restaurant Café-Restaurant**
Address:13 Eratosthenous str, Pangrati
Telephone: +30 210 756 2895
Hours: Sat-Mon, Wed & Thurs, 10am-6pm;
      Fri, 10 am-8pm
Web: www.goulandris.gr/en/cafe

Benaki Museum Restaurant
Address: 1 Koumbari and Vasilissis Sofias,
      Kolonaki
Telephone: +30 210 367 1000
Hours: Mon, Wed, Fri & Sat, 10am-6pm;
      Thurs, 10am-11pm;
      Sun, 10am-4pm
Web: www.benaki.gr

Cycladic Café
Address: Neophytou Douka 4, Kolonaki
Telephone: +30 210 722 8321
Hours: Mon, Wed, Fri & Sat, 10am-5pm;
      Thurs, 10am-8pm;Sun, 11am-5pm
Web: www.cycladic.gr

National Archeological Museum
Address: 28 Oktovriou (Patission) 44
Telephone: +30 213 214 4800
Hours: Mon, 1pm-8pm; Tues-Sun, 8am-3pm
Web: www.namuseum.gr

and coffee) is not on par with that at the Acropolis or Benaki museums, the courtyard's silent statues, their beauty still intact after all these centuries, make for exceptionally pleasant dining partners.

OUT OF SIGHT

Downtown's Hidden Bars

Athens is legendary for its nightlife and Greeks love going out till late, even on weeknights. Though the city has bars for every taste, there's always something special about those found by surprise in the least expected locations, sometimes without even a sign on the door...

The subterranean **Speakeasy** opened in downtown Athens near the Parliament after the owners discovered a spacious basement underneath the ground-floor space where they were planning to establish their bar. Once you ring the unmarked bell to be let in, go down the stairs and through a second door into a beautifully designed 1920s-style bar. Every second Thursday, Speakeasy hosts live music nights with different guest bands, typically playing swing or jazz. Things usually start getting very busy after 11 p.m., except on live-music nights, when it can be hopping as early as 9 p.m.

Metamatic: TAF (The Art Foundation) is located in a narrow alley in the Monastiraki flea market area. This historical building, formerly a stables, a women's prison, an apartment and a storage depot, now offers a unique all-day-bar experience. Track down the old wooden door with the small sign next to it that reads "metamatic:taf," then descend the old marble steps into a beautiful courtyard with trees and a modern bar and tables to sit around. In the building's renovated upstairs, you'll find contemporary art on display. Opens daily at 10:30 a.m. for coffee and stays open till late for cocktails.

Cantina Social is located in the Psyri neighborhood, across the street from Monastiraki, in a hidden courtyard at the end of an arcade. For many years, the space served as a traditional neighborhood kafeneio, owned and run by a group of old men. That same crowd still comes here during the day to talk boisterously and sip Greek coffee. After 10 p.m., the scene changes dramatically, with throngs of young people gathering in

the small bar area inside, or outside in the courtyard, where films and shorts are often projected on the walls of the surrounding buildings. Cantina Social hosts great parties, especially in the spring and summer, and it's always open, even in August.

In Stoa Bolani, another arcade close to Syntagma Square, hides **Low Profile**, one of the best whiskey bars in town. This isn't a place for cocktails, it's what Greeks call a *potadiko,* a place for high-quality bourbon or malts, served straight in the proper glasses and treated with respect. The bar has more than 80 quality whiskies, some of which are very rare. During the day, they serve coffee and snacks, including cheese platters that perfectly complement the drinks. Occasionally they organize whiskey tasting nights.

When writing about one of Athens's best old-fashioned bars, it would be easy to throw around words such as "vintage" or "retro,"

but that would be missing the point at **Galaxy**. Remaining unchanged for decades, it is a landmark of Athenian culture, not just some interior decorator's fantasy. Located downtown – not to be confused with the cocktail bar in the Hilton with the same name – Galaxy is hidden inside a stoa on busy Stadiou Street. It's what Greeks like to call an "American bar," a style of big drinking house that opened in Athens after the Second World War.

Cantina Social
Address: Leokoriou 8, Psyri
Telephone: +30 21 0325 1668
Hours: Tue-Sat, 10am-late

Galaxy
Address: Stadiou 10, Downtown
Telephone: +30 21 0322 7733
Hours: Mon-Sat, 5pm-2am

Low Profile
Address: Voulis 7 (Stoa Bolani), Syntagma
Telephone: +30 213 035 2114
          +30 694 605 3115
Hours: Mon-Sat, 11am-3am;
       Sun, 7pm-3am

Metamatic: TAF
Address: Normanou 5, Monastiraki
Telephone: +30 210 323 8757
Hours: 10:30am-3am

Speakeasy
Address: Lekka 13, Syntagma
No telephone
Hours: 9pm-5am or 6am

THE PHYLLOFILES

Best Baklava

In Greece, baklava is sold in most bakeries and pastry shops around the country, even in supermarkets. In Athens, our favorite is undoubtedly made by the legendary **Belle Vue**, an almost-50-year-old pastry shop in Nea Smyrni owned by two Greek families who used to be based in Istanbul. The pastry chef – or "technician," as they call him – is considered one of the best in town. Behind the sparkling-clean counter you can see the immaculate open workshop, where all the magic happens. Among all the different heavenly varieties of baklava they make, the Turkish-style *baklava kuru* stands out, made with pistachios from the island of Aegina, many layers of pastry, a combination of high-quality sheep's and goat's milk butter and a comparatively drier texture ("kuru" means dry in Turkish) to typically syrupy baklava.

Also in Nea Smyrni, on a residential road, is **Maxim**. The Greek family that owns the shop also used to be based in Istanbul and moved to Athens and opened this business in 1983. The shop transports you to another time; it's quite small and modest but filled with an air of nostalgia, which is rare in most pastry shops nowadays. Maxim offers fewer pastry options, but everything is incredibly fresh, including the two types of baklava, one made with pistachios and another with walnuts – both delicious.

Palet, located in the southern suburb Kalamaki, is owned by the Kordelidis family, which used to own a small chocolate factory in Dolapdere, Istanbul. They moved to Athens in 1977 and opened the pastry shop a year later. Second-generation owner Maria Kordelidis keeps the quality of ingredients high and spreads her love and enthusiasm for what they've been making. A recent renovation has made the shop rather fancy and elegant, and a wide selection of desserts and enticing aromas emerge from

the upstairs workshop. Among the traditional Turkish versions of baklava available – all fresh and delightful – the most popular one is called "Baklava Sultan," stuffed with ground pistachios. It is prepared with a special technique so that the pastry gives the impression of raw dough rather than crispy layers of phyllo. To achieve that, it's baked for less time than normal and is made with a thicker sugar syrup, which keeps it moistened and gives it a softer texture.

For a Greek version, try **Metropolitikon** in central Athens,

near Syntagma Square. This third-generation family business opened in 1930 and is notable for its authentic Greek desserts. The amazing Yiannena-style baklava is made with chopped almonds rolled in two different types of pastry with a sugar-honey syrup. It also sells *baklavou* from Lesbos Island; many layers of thin pastry are alternated with layers of finely chopped almonds and soaked with pure honey and orange syrup.

Open since 1915, **Afoi Asimakopouloi** in Exarchia, another third-generation family-owned pastry

shop, is famous for its homemade dairy products, especially its yogurt and butter. The extraordinary quality of that butter is evident in the Greek-style baklava sold here, one with almonds and one with walnuts, both deeply imbued with the fragrance of cinnamon and clove.

Belle Vue
Address: Eleftheriou Venizelou 104,
          Nea Smyrni
Telephone: +30 210 934 4064
Hours: 6:30am-10pm

Maxim
Address: Tsakiroglou 23, Nea Smyrni
Telephone: +30 210 932 4603
Hours: 9:30am-9:30pm

Palet
Address: Kalamakiou 16, Kalamaki
Telephone: +30 210 9828154
Hours: Mon-Sat, 9am-10pm;
       Sun, 10am-10pm

Metropolitikon (Μητροπολιτικόν)
Address: Voulis 39, Plaka
Telephone: +30 210 322 0226
Hours: Mon-Sat, 8am-9pm;
       closed Sundays

Afoi Asimakopouloi (Αφοί
Ασημακόπουλοι)
Address: Charilaou Trikoupi 82, Exarchia
Telephone: +30 210 361 0092
Hours: Mon-Sat, 7am-10pm;
       Sun, 8am-3:30pm

WORDS TO EAT BY

Agora: market

Anthotyro: a type of mild white cheese, similar to ricotta, made from feta whey

Avgolemono: traditional egg and lemon sauce

Dolmades: stuffed grape leaves

Fava: a traditional type of yellow split pea purée (no relation to the fava bean)

Feta: the classic Greek white cheese, traditionally made from a combination of sheep and goat's milk

Frappé: iced and frothed instant coffee

Freddo: a frothed iced espresso, can be topped with frothed milk for a cappuccino

Fournos: bakery

Gemista: stuffed vegetable dish

Glyko tou Koutaliou: "spoon sweets," traditional fruit or vegetable preserves served as a dessert on their own, or used as toppings for yogurt or ice cream

Graviera: Greek gruyere made either of cows, sheep or goat milk or a combination of sheep and goat milk

Gyros: layers of meat (usually pork or chicken) slowly roasted on a vertical spit, then thinly shaved from the sides to serve either wrapped up in or on top of grilled pita bread with onions, tomatoes and yogurt

Horta: wild seasonal weeds or greens, usually boiled, blanched or steamed and dressed with olive oil and lemon juice and often paired with fish and seafood

Kafenio: a traditional all-day venue where they serve coffee, alcohol and meze dishes

Kebab: an Armenian-style sausage-shaped minced meat patty with spices, often served with a yogurt sauce

Keftedes: traditional meatballs

Koulouri: a bread ring covered in sesame seeds, often stuffed with fillings like cheese or olives, typically sold as a street snack

Ladera: classic Greek vegetable dishes cooked with olive oil (ladi=oil)

Mageirio/oinomageirio: establishment specializing in classic Greek cooking, with daily dishes

Manouri: a type of white cheese

Meze: a selection of small dishes to share and usually paired with wine, ouzo, tsipouro/raki or beer

Mezedopoleio: a taverna specializing in meze dishes

Ouzeri or Tsipouradiko: taverna specializing in meze and ouzo or tsipouro

Ouzo: a traditional spirit made of pressed grapes, aniseed and herbs

Pasteli: a traditional snack bar enjoyed in Greece since ancient times made from sesame and honey, sometimes with nuts, dried fruit or spices added

Pita: refers not to bread but rather to savory pie, e.g. Spanakopita (spinach pie) or tyropita (cheese pie)

Psistaria: traditional grill-house

Saganaki: a small special frying or baking pan used to cook a variety of dishes. The best known one abroad is cheese saganaki, but dishes like shrimp saganaki or mussels saganaki are equally popular in Greece.

Souvlaki: Greece's most famous street-food, made of chunks of meat (traditionally pork) on a stick or wrapped in pita bread along with yogurt, sliced tomatoes and onions

Souvlatzidiko: a souvlaki joint

Taverna: a casual eatery, restaurant or tavern

Tsipouro/tsikoudia/raki : a traditional spirit made of the seeds, stems and skin of grapes which are distilled, similar to Italian grappa

Tzatziki: yogurt, cucumber and garlic dip

Zaharoplastio: pastry shop

INDEX

Alphabetically

Bakeries & Pie Shops

Fish & Seafood

Outdoor Seating

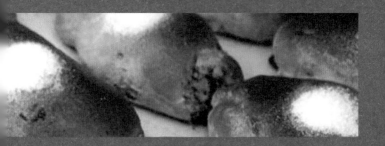

Creative Greek

Mezedopoleio & Tavernas

Bars & Nightlife

Coffee & Desserts

Meat Lovers

Specialty Shops

Greek Classics

Vegetarian Friendly

ATHENS

MAPS

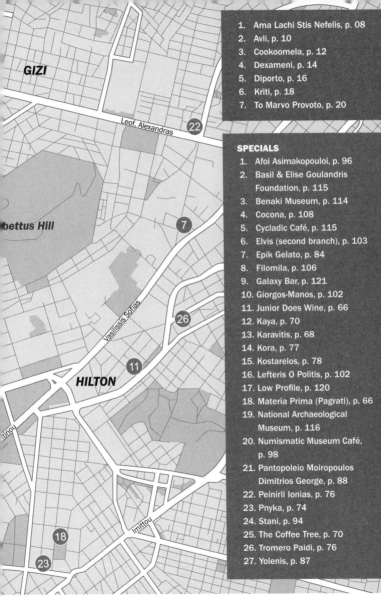

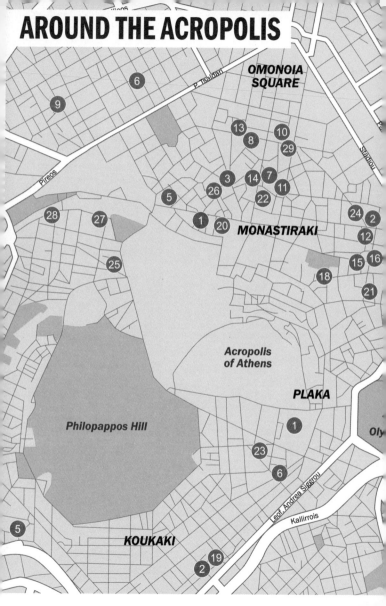

AROUND THE ACROPOLIS

OMONOIA SQUARE

MONASTIRAKI

Acropolis
of Athens

PLAKA

Philopappos Hill

KOUKAKI

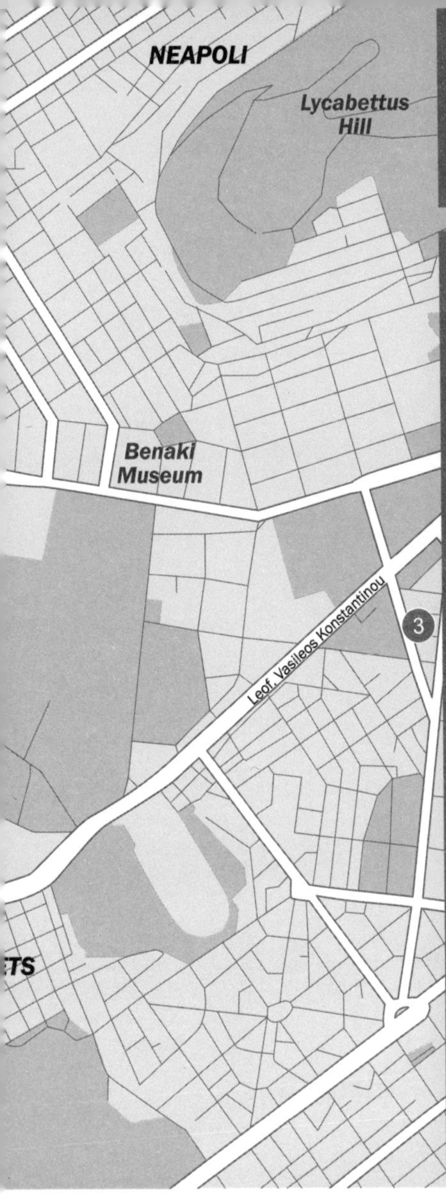

NEAPOLI

Lycabettus
Hill

Benaki
Museum

Leof. Vasileos Konstantinou

③

TS

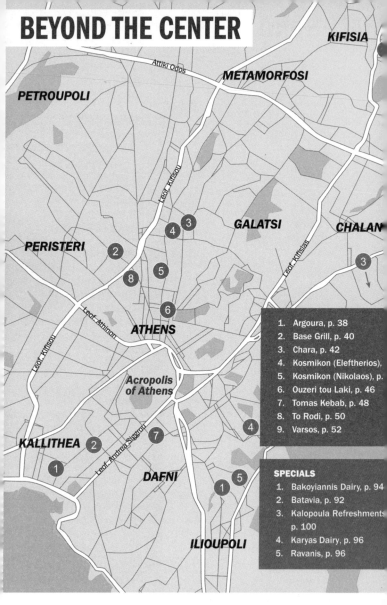

BEYOND THE CENTER

KIFISIA

Attiki Odos

METAMORFOSI

PETROUPOLI

GALATSI

CHALAN

PERISTERI

ATHENS

Acropolis
of Athens

KALLITHEA

DAFNI

ILIOUPOLI

1. Argoura, p. 38
2. Base Grill, p. 40
3. Chara, p. 42
4. Kosmikon (Eleftherios),
5. Kosmikon (Nikolaos), p.
6. Ouzeri tou Laki, p. 46
7. Tomas Kebab, p. 48
8. To Rodi, p. 50
9. Varsos, p. 52

SPECIALS

1. Bakoyiannis Dairy, p. 94
2. Batavia, p. 92
3. Kalopoula Refreshments
   p. 100
4. Karyas Dairy, p. 96
5. Ravanis, p. 96

IRAEUS AND THE DOCKS

MANIATIKA

DRAPETSONA

PIRAEUS

KALLIPOLI

Egaleo

Etolikou

Anapafseos

25'is Martiou

Akti Kondili

Akti Miaouli

Leof. Ir. Politechniou

1. Margaro, p. 56
2. Taxidevontas, p. 58
3. To Eidikon, p. 60

SPECIALS
1. I Feta tis Hiras, p. 79
2. Madras (Piraeus), p. 92
3. Mandragoras, p. 89
4. Stani Kountoura, p. 94

The Global Guide to Local Eats

Culinary Backstreets covers the authentic food scene and offers guided food tours in several of the world's greatest gastro-capitals.

FOOD WALKS!

Explore with Culinary Backstreet:

While the stomach should ideally serve as the best compass, the truth is that it's hard to find your way without good local advice. That's where Culinary Backstreets comes in.

Our small group culinary walks lead you on an educating eating binge through a city's secret side streets and authentic markets, visiting countless hard-to-find culinary gems and, in between bites, untouristed historic monuments. Let us show you the way.

- ▶ ATHENS
- ▶ BARCELONA
- ▶ ISTANBUL
- ▶ LISBON
- ▶ LOS ANGELES
- ▶ MEXICO CITY
- ▶ MARSEILLE
- ▶ NAPLES
- ▶ NEW ORLEANS
- ▶ OAXACA
- ▶ PALERMO
- ▶ PORTO
- ▶ QUEENS
- ▶ TBILISI
- ▶ TOKYO

www.culinarybackstreets.com

culinary backstreets

Athens
An Eater's Guide to the City

Editors: Tas Anjarwalla, Carolina Doriti

Text: Johanna Dimopoulos, Carolina Doriti, Diana Farr Louis, Despina Trivolis and Christiana Thomaidi

Photos: Tas Anjarwalla, Johanna Dimopoulos, Carolina Doriti, Nikos Efstratiadis, Diana Farr Louis, Manteau Stam and Katie Whittaker

Design: Bonnie Briant Design and The Dezine Studio

ISBN 978-0-9863290-1-2

Printed and distributed in Greece by

AGYRA
publications
www.e-agyra.gr